The Apocalypse
of Jesus Christ

The Apocalypse of Jesus Christ

Meditations on Themes from
the Book of Revelation

David Atkinson

WIPF & STOCK · Eugene, Oregon

THE APOCALYPSE OF JESUS CHRIST
Meditations on Themes from the Book of Revelation

Wipf & Stock
An Imprint of Wipf and Stock Publishers
199 W. 8th Ave., Suite 3
Eugene, OR 97401

www.wipfandstock.com

PAPERBACK ISBN: 978-1-7252-6178-5
HARDCOVER ISBN: 978-1-7252-6179-2
EBOOK ISBN: 978-1-7252-6180-8

Manufactured in the U.S.A.   03/20/20

In grateful memory of
Colin Brown
(1932–2019)
Tyndale Hall and Trinity College,
Bristol and Fuller Seminary, Pasadena.
Tutor, supervisor, and friend.

Contents

Preface

THE STRANGE BOOK OF Revelation, written in about AD 95, opens up a world in which Christian people were under threat from the Roman Empire; some were suffering for their faith. Was it easier to fall in with the ways of the empire in all its wealth and prosperity, in spite of its cruelty, than to hold fast to the faith? The prophet John records some visions of the Risen Jesus, which open up for him what we may call "God's perspectives" on the Christian assemblies and on the idolatrous empire in which they found themselves. Written in the sort of poetic literature sometimes called "apocalyptic," and drawing heavily on themes from the Hebrew Bible, John conveys his message encouraging the Christians to stay strong in their witness, while at the same time opening up the demonic realities behind the workings of totalitarian Empire. He looks towards God's ultimate victory over all that is evil in the establishment of God's kingdom. The book is essentially a series of revelations about Jesus Christ: He is the Lord of the Church and King of all creation. He is the Faithful Witness to God's truth, and the Righteous Judge. He is the Beginning and the End of all things.

Today we are subject to the allurements of many different sorts of godless "empires," tempting us to put other gods in the place of Jesus Christ. These may be political or financial, local or global; they may be institutions or ideologies.

These meditations started as a series of Lent talks in 2019 to Churches Together in Sanderstead and Purley, a group of Christian

Churches in South London. Our question was: can the Book of Revelation encourage us in our struggles and our Christian witness in our very different world?

Acknowledgments

I am very grateful to the leadership of Churches Together in the Sanderstead and Purley area in South London for their invitation to give five Lent addresses on the Book of Revelation in March and April 2019, and for the stimulating responses of those who took part.

In particular I thank The Revd. Jeremy Groombridge, CB, assistant priest at All Saints Church, Sanderstead, for his administrative help with the Lent Addresses, and for his constant support, friendship, and encouragement.

I am also grateful to Dr. Mark Bredin for his careful reading of my typescript, and for numerous constructive suggestions—many of which I have adopted.

Apocalypse

The Book of Revelation

WE HAVE ALL SEEN a political cartoon. There are examples of Donald Trump dressed as a bald eagle representing America, having dealings with Vladimir Putin, depicted as a bear, a historic symbol of Russia. Way back in 1945, the final year of World War II, when Churchill and Stalin and Roosevelt met at Yalta, there were cartoons of a British lion, a bear, and a bald eagle trying to talk to each other. The leaders of three great powers were deciding world history. Some years ago, I saw a cartoon called "Cold War," which showed the eagle and the bear shouting at each other across a huge abyss. We know what these cartoons mean: strangely drawn symbolic creatures stand for political ideologies or for world rulers. Sometimes they also stand for the demonic energy behind world powers. That is what political cartoons are so good at exposing. And that is the sort of symbolic world into which the Book of Revelation draws us. Revelation is a strange book, with wars and bloodshed, empires, kings and nations, dragons and monsters, angels, trumpets, and bowls of wrath. Many people have wondered what it is doing in a Christian Bible. Is there any Christian gospel there at all?

Only one century or so after the Book of Revelation was written, these very questions were being asked, prompting a response
from Dionysius, Bishop of Alexandria. He commented that some
Christians even before his time had "rejected the book," declaring
it to be "unintelligible and illogical." "But for my part," he goes on,
"I should not dare to reject the book, since many brethren hold it
in estimation; but, reckoning that my perception is inadequate to
form an opinion concerning it, I hold that the interpretation of
each several passage is in some way hidden and more wonderful.
For even although I do not understand it, yet I suspect that some
deeper meaning underlies the words."[1] Over the centuries since,
there has been much scholarly and devotional care given to the
"hidden" and "wonderful" things Revelation has to say, and many
of its "deeper meanings" have been uncovered. Much may remain
"unintelligible and illogical," but many Christians—especially
those suffering under oppressive regimes—have found in its message a word of encouragement and hope, whereas for others, the
warnings about the seductions of Empire have come as a call for
repentance and renewal.

The Book of Revelation includes many strange symbolic creatures, which contribute to the vision that John the author has experienced and is recording. It is not easy to interpret every detail;
much more important is to catch in our imaginations the impact
of the visions themselves. But one thing is clear. Revelation is, in
part at least, a book about power: the power of Empire—particularly the Roman Empire at the time the book was written, about
AD 95, when Domitian was the emperor. But, as we shall discover,
Revelation is also and much more significantly about the power
of Jesus Christ—a power, in his case, not of coercive violence, but
of self-giving sacrifice and love, a divine power which ultimately
defeats and destroys every power of evil. Domitian, like other em-
perors before him, demanded the worship of his citizens. The Roman Empire was an idolatrous and tyrannical regime. Only thirty
years earlier, Christians were persecuted, sometimes martyred,
under Nero. Within living memory, Palestine had been captured

1. Dionysius, "Revelation," 271.

by the Roman armies under Vespasian, the temple destroyed, and its treasures stolen and taken to Rome by General Titus. When John, our author, was writing, it was a difficult time for Christian churches, and John was well aware of their struggles. Was there more persecution and martyrdom on the horizon? Certainly there were pressures to conform to the values of the secular world around them, leading sometimes to loss of faith and sometimes to complacency and self-satisfaction. It was also written to encourage them in their struggles in the context of an idolatrous empire, to strengthen their faith in a time of tribulation, and to warn them from being seduced by the allurements of the powerful but godless culture around them. That can be oppressive in its own way, but sometimes simply falling in with the "ways of the world" can be easier than suffering active persecution.

Quite often, when people are oppressed by a tyrannical or totalitarian regime, there emerges a resistance movement that produces its own literature—a sort of underground newspaper. In the culture of the Jewish people, they had at times produced a distinctive sort of literature to strengthen their faith and encourage them in their struggles. It came to be called apocalyptic literature. We find it in the strange visions described in the Book of Ezekiel at the time of the exile in the sixth century BC, and most notably in the second half of the Book of Daniel and in the oracles of the prophet Zechariah. The author of Daniel sets his book way back at the time of the exile but in a way that reflects on the suffering of his own time under Antiochus Epiphanes in about 164 BC. "Apocalyptic literature" is specially written for people who are oppressed, or vulnerable or afraid, or in danger of giving up on their faith. It is a sort of underground literature of liberation telling you what is really going on behind the scenes, to keep your spirits up and to subvert the enemy. It is about uncovering the truth that you might need to face if you are to avoid the seductions of imperial power.

During the Second World War, an "underground press" appeared in France, Belgium, Norway, Denmark, the Nether-lands—indeed, I think in every country that was occupied by Nazi Germany. Its aim was to raise morale, to intensify the will of the people to resist, to provide a forum for discussing the goals to be aimed for after liberation. Similarly, Jewish "apocalyptic literature" was intended to encourage endurance in resistance to the powers of the world that were threatening God's people. And, as we have said, one of the features of John's day was pressure from the Roman Empire within which the small Christian assemblies were set. Sadly, life was actually sometimes easier for Christians if they fell in with the ways of the empire.

In the Book of Revelation, the author John draws on some of the apocalyptic symbolism which we find in visions in the prophecies of Ezekiel and Daniel about the oppressive regimes of their times. John's purpose is to strengthen and warn his friends and acquaintances in the Christian churches, living in his day under the allurements of Rome, to urge them to keep their faith in Christ. John also alludes to many other prophets, to many of the psalms, and especially to the story of the exodus: Moses leading God's people away from slavery under the oppressive regime of Pharaoh and towards liberation in the promised land.

In our world, we also know about oppressive, seductive totalitarian power, whether Hitler's fascism, Stalin's state socialism, or the power of other destructive and divisive corporate institutions and ideologies. We, too, know the "oppression"—often subconsciously—of the allurements of secular culture around us, drawing us away from a radical commitment to Jesus Christ. It is very significant that when Pope Francis in his 2015 Encyclical *Laudato Si'* referred to the Market System that holds so much of our world's politics in thrall today, he tellingly called it "the deified Market."[2] He is not, of course, criticizing markets and methods of trade as such; he is opposed to "the Market" ideology, which seems to override any human powers to control it, and which is geared not to human values but to the assumption of limitless economic growth, which results in everything and everyone being reduced to a commodity with a price tag. The Pope sees the Market as one of today's idols or false gods, which, alongside idolatrous nationalisms and what Eisenhower once called "the military-industrial

2. Francis, *Laudato Si'*, 31.

complex," not to mention the threats of nuclear war or the specters of environmental devastation and extinction caused by climate change, creates divisions, fears, and destructive tensions. The Book of Revelation may very well give us a fresh perspective on the "Empires" of our world.

It may also have things to say to us about the struggles of trying to live faithful lives in a godless context, about the suffering for their faith of Christians in too many parts of the world where persecution is real and strong, and how to cope in response to the systematic destruction of Christian churches by various anti-Christian groups. It may also shake us out of the complacency of thinking all is well when Christian groups and Christian disciples are losing their bearings in an oppressive culture of godless values and apparently attractive allurements towards worldly satisfactions which displace the lordship of Christ.

So, in the Book of Revelation, we have the symbolism of political cartoons exposing political powers. We have apocalyptic writing encouraging suffering and unwary Christians to stand firm in their faith. And we also have something more. For what was most puzzling for suffering Christians was this: Had not Jesus taught his disciples about the coming kingdom of God's rule of justice and of peace? Had not Jesus promised that he would come again and take them to himself? Had he not said, "Do not let your hearts be troubled, neither let them be afraid"? And now this! Where was God in all the persecutions and allurements of Roman Empire? Where were the signs of God's coming kingdom? Where was Jesus, whom they knew had died on a Roman cross, but whom God had raised to life again in a new creation on Easter morning? How were they to hold on to their faith when the political context did everything it could to make living faithfully very difficult, and when the consumerist culture around all too readily exposed the realities of human greed? How were they to live humanly and for God in this fallen world? John, the author of Revelation, is addressing just these sorts of questions. And he does so because these are very personal questions also for him. Through his sufferings he had learned more about that very different power: the power of

God's suffering love, seen in Jesus' death and resurrection, which confronts evil in creative, healing, and life-giving judgment.

1. John: "On Patmos . . . In the Spirit."

This is what John tells us:

> I, John, your brother who share with you in Jesus *the persecution and the kingdom and the patient endurance,* was on the island called Patmos because of the word of God and the testimony of Jesus. I was in the Spirit on the Lord's day, and I heard behind me a loud voice like a trumpet, saying, "Write in a book what you see, and send it to the seven churches." (Rev 1:9–11, emphasis added)

John was on the island of Patmos, a few miles out from the coast of what we now call Turkey. He was in exile there because of his faith, his preaching of the word of God, and his testimony to Jesus. He, too, had suffered at the hands of the Roman Empire. And John tells his brothers and sisters that he shares with them in Jesus "the persecution and the kingdom, and the patient endurance." We shall find these three themes woven throughout the Book of Revelation. We will be reminded that Jesus himself faced tribulation—persecution and torture leading to crucifixion. And he prepared his followers: "In the world you face tribulation/persecution. But take courage, I have conquered the world!" (John 16:33).

Jesus also taught his followers about God's kingdom, and himself as the coming King. "Strive first for the kingdom of God and his righteousness, and all else you need will be given to you as well" (Matt 6:33). He also spoke of the new world of God's future: "Truly I tell you, at the renewal of all things, when the Son of Man is seated on the throne of his glory, you who have followed me will also sit on twelve thrones, judging the twelve tribes of Israel" (Matt 19:28).

The call to follow Christ with patience and persistent obedience is another theme that recurs through the Book of Revelation. It became a favorite theme in the early years of Christian faith: it meant continuing with Christ in his suffering and tribulation.

Christian faith is never easy. The calling is to follow Christ in his path of obedience to the Father's will, share in his sufferings, and so share in his glory and his throne.

John was an exile on Patmos. But he was also "in the Spirit," aware that apart from the rocks and raging sea around him, apart from the Roman power of those who had imprisoned him, there was a whole spiritual realm which we mostly cannot see. Heaven is God's realm of being and activity, but it is not separate from earth. Heaven is the largely unseen part of God's creation that gives meaning to what goes on here and now on earth. These two phrases—"on Patmos" and "in the Spirit"—help us keep our bearings throughout our readings in the Book of Revelation. "On Patmos": part of the suffering church trying to live humanly following Christ in this world; "in the Spirit": open to God and to the heavenly realities which give this earthly life its meaning and its goal.

In G. K. Chesterton's novel *The Man Who was Thursday*, a person called Syme says this:

> "Shall I tell you the secret of the whole world? It is that we have only known the back of the world. We see everything from behind, and it looks brutal. That is not a tree, but the back of a tree. That is not a cloud but the back of a cloud. Cannot you see that everything is stooping and hiding a face? If only we could get round in front."[3]

The Book of Revelation takes us round in front. And it does so through these visions given to John. John seems to be one of some recognized prophets in the church of that time, and he presents his record of his visions from the risen Jesus as words of prophecy for the whole church. They are written as a circular letter to the local churches of Asia Minor of that time, but they are in effect a general letter carrying a word from God for all Christians at all times. This is the starting point for our contemporary reading of this strange book. It addresses the prayers and tears of persecuted and oppressed Christians in today's world, and it rebukes the weakness of faith and lack of love in today's church and calls

---

3. Chesterton, *Thursday*, 170.

us to repentance and endurance. The Book of Revelation is not a foretelling of future events, but a prophetic word for Ephesus and Laodicea and the other churches in the area, and therefore a prophetic word also for us and the world-wide church today. The fact that there are seven churches—and the number seven usually refers to "completeness"—suggests that the whole church, in its entirety, world-wide and history-long, is in view. John says that his words are intended to be read aloud in the context of public worship (1:3). Indeed, as we shall see, in one sense the whole book is ultimately about worship. Twice we read of John falling down in worship at the feet of an angel messenger to be told that he must rather "worship God" (Rev 19:10; 22:9).

What John sees and hears comes from the God whom we describe as the Holy Trinity, Father, Son, and Holy Spirit. John refers to God the Father as "he who is," described as "the Alpha and the Omega, who was and who is and who is to come, the Almighty" (1:8). God is the Beginning and the End of all history. God's word comes in Jesus, "the faithful witness, the first born from the dead and [with reference to Psalm 89:27], the ruler of the kings of the earth" (1:5). God's word comes in the power of "the seven spirits before the throne"—that is God's Holy Spirit (1:4). The word comes through his angel to John, who himself is to pass it on as a prophetic word to the churches—and they in their turn are to be faithful witnesses to Jesus. Several times the Book of Revelation is called a "prophecy"—but not in the sense of telling the future. Revelation is not a sort of holy horoscope, and we get into all sorts of trouble if we try to understand it as a prediction of what is going to happen in the political world, as too many of today's popular paperbacks try to do. Revelation is prophecy in the sense that it is a powerful word from God and about God's purposes for the world: God's word is addressed here and now on earth.

At the center of all that John sees and hears is Jesus Christ. The very first verse of the book gives us the clue: "The Apocalypse of Jesus Christ." "Apocalypse" means "unveiling," "disclosure," "revelation," "bringing into the light what has been hidden." The whole book of Revelation is a disclosure, a revelation of Jesus

Christ, giving us, so to speak, "God's perspectives" on things: God's perspectives on the church; God's perspectives on pagan Empire. The phrase "apocalypse of Jesus Christ" means both that the revelation comes *from* Jesus Christ, often by way of his angelic messengers, and also that it is a revelation *about* Jesus Christ. It is Jesus Christ who becomes the primary subject of the book from the first chapter onwards.

2. "The Apocalypse of Jesus Christ"

The risen Jesus lifts the veil which hides God's secret purposes in history and opens a door from this material world into heaven so that John can see through to what is really going on behind the scenes. We have here both a "self-revelation" of God, and a disclosure of what we may call "God's view from heaven" of the world, the evils which afflict it and its need for healing and renewal. We must not imagine heaven to be away from this world up above the clouds. No. Heaven is the realm of God's action here. Heaven is as close as you and me, but we only get glimpses every now and then. In the Hebrew Bible the prominent meeting place of heaven and earth was the temple. There, particularly in the Holy of Holies, heaven and earth come together. In the New Testament we discover that Jesus was, in person, God's temple, the place where heaven and earth meet. In God's purposes, heaven and earth belong together, and in Jesus we get the clearest glimpse of that. The Book of Revelation refers many times to the significance of the temple. What happens on earth affects what happens in heaven. And what happens in heaven affects what happens on earth. Both are aspects of God's created world.

So the Book of Revelation is essentially about Jesus—the man from Galilee who lived among us, and who suffered great tribulation, was crucified, and whom God raised from death: Jesus, the Son of God, "the faithful witness," who is alive, "the firstborn from the dead," and is now at the center of heaven, and "ruler of the kings of the earth" (1:5).

In his opening paragraph, John reflects on what Jesus has done for us: he loves us, he freed us from our sins through his death on the cross, and he has made us to be a kingdom of priests serving God the Father.

> To him who loves us and freed us from our sins by his blood, and made us to be a kingdom, priests serving his God and Father, to him be glory and dominion forever and ever. Amen. (Rev 1:5–6)

The first thing that John emphasizes is that Jesus loves us. And we need to hold on to that, especially when we get caught up into some of the more gruesome chapters later in the Book of Revelation. We will read of many evil things: evil monsters and evil powers and their destructiveness and seductiveness; and we will hear of God's righteous judgments against all that is evil, and God's care for and liberation of his suffering people. But the first word, and the overarching word, is love. We may recall the reflection from the writer of Deuteronomy on God's rescue of his people from slavery in Egypt:

> It was not because you were more numerous than any other people that the Lord set his heart on you and chose you—for you were the fewest of all peoples. It was *because the Lord loved you* and kept the oath that he swore to your ancestors, that the Lord has brought you out with a mighty hand, and redeemed you from the house of slavery, from the hand of Pharaoh king of Egypt. Know therefore that the Lord your God is God, the faithful God who maintains covenant loyalty with those who love him and keep his commandments. (Deut 7:7–9, emphasis added)

John uses many of these exodus themes throughout the Book of Revelation: in the context of God's covenant promise to Abraham and his family, and looking back also to the story of Noah and God's covenant with the whole of creation, God calls Moses to lead God's people from slavery, to set them free to serve him as a new community in a new land. In John's mind this is all summarized in the phrase, "Jesus freed us from our sins through his blood shed on the cross." And then he goes on: "he made us to be a kingdom of priests." This image also comes from the exodus story. After the people had been rescued from the tyranny of Pharaoh and set free on Passover night from Egypt, they passed through the waters of the Red Sea and started their pilgrimage through the wilderness. They came to Mount Sinai, where Moses was to receive the Ten Commandments, but first the Lord called to Moses from the mountain:

> "Thus you shall say to the house of Jacob, and tell the Israelites: You have seen what I did to the Egyptians, and how I bore you on eagles' wings and brought you to myself. Now therefore, if you obey my voice and keep my covenant, you shall be my treasured possession out of all the people. Indeed the whole earth is mine, but you shall be for me a priestly kingdom and a holy nation. These are the words that you shall speak to the Israelites." (Exod 19:3–6)

God promises that his people shall be a kingdom of priests, in other words, that God's people are to share in God's kingly rule of care and protection for the whole of creation and, with priestly access to God's presence, are to be mediators between God and God's world. That promise does not find its fulfillment throughout all the ups and downs of the history of God's people—until now. Now on Patmos, John in his vision can see the fulfillment of God's promises: for the whole of history, for the whole of creation, for all God's people. They are promises that express God's love, seen supremely in the self-giving love of Jesus Christ on the cross. God's people are to share in Christ's reign, being witnesses to God's ways to the world so that—using the testimony of God's people in the power of God's Spirit—God in his love will liberate and heal. Even "the nations" and the "kings of the earth" (a phrase we will meet many times) are brought under the rule of Christ. All the sufferings of God's people under Pharaoh, in exile in Babylon, under Antiochus Epiphanes, and now under Nero and Domitian, find their meaning and their redemption through the shed blood of Christ, through Christ's victory over evil, and through the gift of Christ's risen life in the Spirit.

To a persecuted and suffering church, John's message is: Do not lose heart; there is more going on in the world than you can easily discern. God has purposes for the whole of God's creation that you do not know. You and your sufferings and struggles are all caught up into that bigger story of God's purposes for history. Your sufferings and struggles are heard in heaven. If we have ever asked "Where are you, Lord?" or echoed the cry of the Psalmist, "O Lord, how long?" then John's visions and prophecy have things to say to us. This book is the Revelation of Jesus Christ—about the disclosure and unveiling of Jesus Christ, living and reigning "on earth as in heaven."

As we progress through the Book of Revelation, we see aspects of that disclosure in a series of visions which is not like normal history in which one thing happens after another. They are much more like a kaleidoscope in which different pieces come into focus at different moments, or perhaps like a cinema film using a split screen with several things happening at once. Although the visions are recorded as happening in sequence in time, we are taken outside our time into God's "time," and we discover that some of the visions seem to be cycles of events that repeat the same message, but from different perspectives. We will meet some horrible monsters in our political cartoon, and also many numbers. John seems to spend a lot of time and care on getting his numbers right. His is a very carefully crafted record. The numbers mean important things for him and for his hearers. We come across four winds, four horsemen, four living creatures. "Four" seems to be about the whole world: north, south, east, and west. And there are lots of sevens: seven golden lampstands (which we find means seven churches), seven stars, seven letters, a scroll with seven seals, seven angels with seven trumpets, seven bowls of wrath, and the "seven spirits" which is a way of speaking of the Holy Spirit. "Seven" seems to signify completeness. There are also numerous quotations from the Old Testament. We have already noted the reference to the exodus story and to visions in Ezekiel and Daniel. There are very many such allusions and quotations. In fact almost every verse in Revelation has some allusion to or quotation from the Hebrew Bible—so if there is something that seems very obscure, the chances are that it is a quotation from Daniel or Ezekiel or Jeremiah, or from Isaiah or the Psalms. Part of John's purpose is to bring all these Hebrew images and symbols and prophecies into their proper focus in the life and death of Jesus, and in his continuing ministry as Risen Lord through the Spirit—as if to say that all the Hebrew Bible finds its fulfillment in Jesus.

Throughout, we shall constantly find that things in this world are not always as they seem to our limited sight. We will hear suffering people offering prayers to God, which do not seem to be answered, only to find that they are taken up into God's purposes as a powerful tool in God's judgments against evil. We are told of "kings of the earth" who seem to exercise power against God, and yet in the end we discover that they have their place within God's kingdom. We will meet the Beast (a symbol of the Roman Empire), which seems to be in control, but we find that in God's purposes, it is eventually defeated through its own self-destruction. Seeming defeat for God and God's people becomes, throughout the book, the story of the triumph of the Crucified Christ and the renewal of all things in God's kingdom.

In our series of reflections and studies, we will pick up some major themes from the Book of Revelation; a convenient way of dividing the material is by focusing on sections which cover successively seven letters, seven seals, seven trumpets, and seven bowls of God's wrath, leading ultimately to a glorious vision of the whole of creation healed and renewed. Throughout all this we find a progressive disclosure of Jesus Christ. He is presented to us throughout the book as:

- The Risen Lord of the church, giving warning, rebuke, and encouragement (Rev 1–3);

- The crucified Lamb, the Lord of history, opening the seven seals of God's book of world destiny and plan of salvation (Rev 4:1—8:5);

- The King of all creation—seven trumpets sound a call to repentance from a broken world, and a call to realize that

Christ has already begun his reign over all other spiritual powers (Rev 8:6—11:19);

- The Victorious Word; the Faithful and True Witness; and the Righteous Judge, as God's seven bowls of wrath destroy all the powers of evil behind worldly empires; (Rev 12:1—20:15);

- The Lord of Life: the Beginning and the End, and the Coming One (Rev 21:1—22:5).

Whatever else is happening in the world, Jesus Christ is Lord. It is this picture of the Sovereign Lord of heaven and earth, the faithful and loving Lord of the church, the Crucified Lamb, now risen from the dead, which we must keep in mind when we hear every cry of suffering, see every bloody battle, and experience every catastrophe of which the later chapters speak.

But there are also interludes in the story in which we hear how God's faithful servants are kept safe. We hear of the power of their prayers and we understand the significance of their witness and their preaching, until at last, in John's vision, with the last trumpet the kingdom of this world becomes the kingdom of God, and God's people, a kingdom of priests, are given their share in Christ's reign on earth. All the forces that were intent on destroying the earth are removed. God's sanctuary in heaven is opened. Everything leads towards the wonderful final two chapters of the Book of Revelation in which John is given a vision of a new heaven and a new earth, a new people, a New Jerusalem. There God says, "Behold, I make all things new." And the Risen Jesus says, "Behold, I am coming soon!"

The following outline gives the shape of our book.

The Apocalypse of Jesus Christ

I, John, your brother who share with you in Jesus the tribulation and the kingdom and the patient endurance, was on the island called Patmos because of the word of God and the testimony of Jesus. I was in the Spirit on the Lord's day, and I heard behind me a loud voice like a trumpet, saying, "Write in a book what you see, and send it to the seven churches." (Rev 1:9–11)

1: (Rev 1–3) The Risen Jesus is Lord of the Church.

1:1–8 Opening greetings.

1:9–20 John's vision of the Risen Jesus, and Jesus' commission to John to write what he sees.

2:1—3:22 *Seven messages* from the Risen Jesus to the seven churches of Asia Minor: Do not lose your love, keep faithful, beware of ungodly powers, wake up, keep patient, hold on in faith.

2: (Rev 4:1—8:5) The Crucified Lamb Is the Lord of History.

4:1—5:14 The throne room of heaven. The Lamb is worthy to open the *seven seals* of God's scroll of world history and destiny.

6:1–17 The Lamb opens six of the seven seals, revealing ungodly powers at work in the world: conquest, war, injustice, famine, deadly pestilence.

7:1–17 Multitudes from every nation receive God's protection in their tribulation.

8:1–5. The seventh seal is opened. Heaven is silent. A call to realize the power of prayer.

3: (Rev 8:6—11:19) Jesus is King of All Creation.

8:6—9:21 Angels blow six of their *seven trumpets*, warning of devastation to God's creation, and calling for repentance.

10:1–11 The angel with the little scroll tells John he must prophesy. A call to preach.

11:1–14 God's people are protected. Two witnesses urge them to be strong.

11:15–19 The last trumpet is sounded. The kingdom of the world becomes the kingdom of God. Those who destroy God's earth are destroyed. God's sanctuary in heaven is opened.

4: (Rev 12:1—20:15) Jesus is Victorious Word, Faithful Witness, Righteous Judge.

12:1—14:20 A war in heaven: Satan at war with the church. A call for endurance. The Dragon, the Beast of imperial pagan power, and the False Prophet form a parody of Trinity. The Lamb is triumphant on Mount Zion. God's people "follow the Lamb wherever he goes."

15:1—16:21 God's people sing "the song of Moses and of the Lamb." *Seven bowls of God's wrath* release God's final judgments against evil.

17:1—19:10 "Babylon," the city of Mammon, falls. The Marriage Feast of the Lamb. Hallelujah!

19:11—20:15 The final victories over all evil. The death of Death.

5: (Rev 19:11—22:5) Jesus is Lord of Life: the Beginning and the End.

All things are made new: a new heaven, a new earth, a New Jerusalem. All creation is healed, and God and the Lamb receive the worship of all creation.

(22:6–21 Epilogue: Jesus says "I am coming soon").

1

The Risen Jesus Is Lord of the Church

(Rev 1:10—3:22)

1. John's Vision of the Risen Jesus

I was in the Spirit on the Lord's day, and I heard behind me a loud voice like a trumpet, saying, "Write in a book what you see and send it to the seven churches: to Ephesus, to Smyrna, to Pergamum, to Thyatira, to Sardis, to Philadelphia and to Laodicea." Then I turned to see whose voice it was that spoke to me. And on turning I saw seven golden lampstands, and in the midst of the lampstands I saw one like the Son of Man, clothed with a long robe and with a golden sash across his chest. His head and his hair were white as white wool, white as snow; his eyes were like a flame of fire, his feet were like burnished bronze, refined as in a furnace, and his voice was like the sound of many waters. In his right hand he held seven stars, and from his mouth came a sharp two-edged sword, and his face was like the sun shining in full force. When I saw him, I fell at his feet as though dead. But he placed his right hand on me saying, "Do not be afraid; I am the first and the last, and the living one. I was dead, and see, I am alive forever and ever; and I have the keys of Death and of Hades. Now write what you have

> seen, what is, and what is to take place after this . . . the
> seven stars are the angels of the seven churches, and the
> seven lampstands are the seven churches." (1:10–20)

THIS IS VERY LIKE a description, in places almost word for word, of the Son of Man in the Book of Daniel chapter 7, and also from another vision in Daniel chapter 10. In Daniel 7, the visions provide various depictions of God on the throne surrounded by attendants. They take place on earth and show God's majesty and holiness and power. There are hints of the creation narrative in Genesis, and of God's redemption of his people at the exodus. The history of the nations is unfolded, and a human-like figure ("one like the Son of Man") emerges who implements the rule of God on earth, in place of a tyrannical empire of idolatrous power. Many Christians have interpreted these visions in Daniel in the light of the coming of Jesus Christ. John does that here:

> "Look! He is coming with the clouds; every eye shall see
> him, even those who pierced him; and on his account all
> the tribes of the earth will wail. (Rev 1:7)

In John's vision in Revelation chapter 1, the risen Jesus is seen "like the Son of Man, clothed with a long robe and with a golden sash on his chest" (1:13). Perhaps this depicts Jesus as a priest—certainly as a leader. His eyes are like fire, seeing through all falsehood, his voice is like the sound of many waters, refreshing and life-giving, his mouth a two-edged sword—a word with which he confronts evil—and his face shining like the sun. And Jesus is walking among the lampstands (*seven lampstands* means *seven churches*—1:20). He is "in the midst of the churches": he identifies with the churches and is familiar with them; he knows their strengths and weaknesses and their needs.

John places this vision of Christ at the very start of his book. John heard Jesus speaking, then says, "When I saw him, I fell at his feet . . . But he placed his right hand on me, saying 'Do not be afraid. I am the First and the Last'" (1:17–18). Jesus is "the living one; dead, but now alive for evermore. He has the keys of Death and of Hades." In other words, Jesus has authority over life and over death. Jesus also picks up the words used of God Almighty, the Alpha and the Omega (1:8), and describes himself as "the First and the Last"—the beginning and source and goal and meaning of all things. Jesus then says to John: "Now write what you have seen, what is, and what is to take place after this"—bear witness to what God is doing. You, John, are to be a faithful witness too.

2. Seven Messages from the Risen Jesus to the Churches.

John is told to write seven prophetic messages from the Risen Jesus, one for each of the seven churches of Asia Minor. Each church has its *angel*, depicted as a star—perhaps the spiritual nature of each church is somehow represented in heaven by its angel? Each letter is written to one of the churches, and together they make up one circular letter for all the churches. It is also clear that each prophetic message is addressed to the whole church. Each church receives all seven letters. *Seven*, we said, stands for completeness: these messages are for all the churches, for then and for now. Each letter describes some feature of the Risen Jesus, and it is not until we have read all seven that the full portrait we were given earlier is made clear. Only when all the churches are seen together is the whole Christ made visible.

Jesus most often first finds something to praise about the church, and then there is a "however." Then there are words of rebuke and warning: there are things you as a church need to do if you are going to hold fast to your faith and to pull through times of temptation, and even times of possible impending catastrophe. There are also words of encouragement and blessing. Here, then, are the seven letters to the local assemblies. Quite often they make sobering reading. But the good news is that very soon—in Revelation chapter 4—we are allowed to see through heaven's open door, and that vision will be joyous and filled with hope.

(i) The First Letter Is to the Church in Ephesus (2:1–7).

Jesus is described as one who holds the seven stars in his hand (which I think means that he guides and directs his angels) and who walks among the golden lampstands. Jesus is a living presence among the churches. The Risen Jesus is alive and walking in the midst of the Christian communities: what does he find there?

Ephesus is the metropolitan center, the most important city on our list, with the great temple to Artemis (Diana), which was one of the wonders of the ancient world. So it was also a religious center. "I know your works, your toil and your patient endurance." Your sufferings and struggles are known in heaven. But—and it is a big "but"—you have lost your first love. How very far you have fallen! There are Nicolaitans among you: people who get caught up into the worship of the Roman Emperor. They have become insidious half-believers: a sort of fifth column who damage the church from the inside. Jesus says: I know that you have been testing out those who seem to be true believers but are not. However, your narrow inquisitorial spirit and zeal for truth and for orthodoxy have crowded out love. So "keep on remembering your first love." Without love you really cease to be church at all—you will have your lampstand taken away. Listen to the Spirit. The Church of England clergyman John Stott used to pray that Christians "be given grace not to forsake truth because of the shallowness of our love, nor to forsake love because of the narrowness of our truth."[1] Those who *overcome* or *conquer* (that is by faithful following of Jesus and bearing witness to him) will have the *right to eat from the tree of life in the paradise of God*—a tree first mentioned in the Garden of Eden, and which appears again in the vision of the new heaven and new earth in Revelation chapter 21.

(ii) The Second Letter Is to *Smyrna* (2:8–11).

Smyrna was one of the greatest cities of the region and known for its beauty. It had been destroyed in c. 600 BC, and then rebuilt. So

---

1. A prayer the author heard Stott pray from the pulpit many times.

it is apt that the description of the Risen Jesus in this letter is "the first and the last, who was dead and came to life." Jesus has nothing but praise for the Christians of Smyrna. He knows that they have suffered. And they are going to be tested again. God does not always keep his people from poverty, or from persecution. Yet God gives grace to endure, and the way the assembly in Smyrna have handled their poverty and affliction makes them rich in his eyes. (Sadly, there is a phrase in this letter that has too often been used in later years, even our own time, in an anti-Semitic way. It seems there were some people who had taken over control of the Jewish synagogue, although they were not faithful Jews at all but were collaborators with the Romans. These imposters are here called "a synagogue of Satan"—but that is not a phrase that should ever have been used in general terms of Jewish people, although shamefully too often it has.) Jesus' words to the suffering people of Smyrna were to keep going: "Be faithful until death, and I will give you the crown of life." Those who overcome will not be harmed but will be part of the great resurrection when the Lord comes in glory.

(iii) Letter Number Three Is for the Church in *Pergamum* (2:12–17).

Pergamum was a center of local government, and the capital of an independent province established after Alexander the Great. It had a great and famous library. It was known as a multicultural center of many religious and political groups. It was a preeminent center for the worship of Caesar, the Roman Emperor. The trouble was that there was too much cultural assimilation of other beliefs and values getting into the church. Jesus is described as holding a "two-edged sword," his word of truth (1:16), dividing truth from error. This is a powerful image in a city where the Roman proconsul had the power of the sword. Jesus holds another power—the word of God, greater than any earthly power. Although many in Pergamum, Jesus says, held fast to his name and did not deny their faith in him, even when one of their company had been martyred, others had fallen into the error of Balaam in leading people astray from God's ways. The strange story of Balaam in the Old Testament (Num 22–25 and 31:16) had become a byword for spiritual backsliding. The Nicolaitans with their worship of the Roman Emperor as a god were apparently a factor in Pergamum as well. The church in Pergamum needs to be much more discerning and weigh everything in the light of Jesus' word of truth. The faithful will receive a white stone, which might possibly refer to an acquittal in a law court, or even a token of entry to a feast—in this case the coming banquet of God.

(iv) The Fourth Letter Is for *Thyatira* (2:18–29).

Thyatira was a small town at the center of the textile trade, with lots of trade guilds. Jesus appears to the church here as the Son of God who has "eyes like a flame of fire, and whose feet are like burnished bronze" (cf. Dan 10:6). They are a faithful, loving, serving, and enduring church, and they need to *hold fast* to the good things they have. Some, however, are guilty of "playing around" with spiritual things as well, tempted to follow the Jezebels of this world into all sorts of ungodly and wicked behavior. Her teaching is false. "Do not go that way," says Jesus. "But if you hold fast and continue to do my works you will receive the morning star"—a name for Jesus himself (Rev 22:16). You will be with Jesus.

(v) Letter Number Five Is about *Sardis* (3:1–6).

The church in Sardis does not seem to have any particular problems, except that it is *dead*! A commercial city, they "had a name for being alive," but had lost their spiritual life. They had settled for mediocrity. Wake up! Remember what you have received and heard; obey it and repent. There are just a few of you who are worthy of wearing white robes—a symbol of new life in Christ. But for the rest: watch out! This is no time for spiritual laziness!

(vi) The Sixth Church Is *Philadelphia* (3:7–13).

This sixth letter is addressed to the church in Philadelphia, which must have been a joy to know. Jesus is "the holy and true one who has the keys of David" (cf. Isaiah 22:22), a symbol, perhaps, of admission to "the City of David," the New Jerusalem, God's home. Jesus recognizes that the church has little power of its own, but they have kept his word with patient endurance and have not denied his name. He loves them. There are more Roman collaborators associated with the synagogue here, but the faithful must hold on to what they have. They will be pillars in God's temple—signs of being firmly in God's presence—with God's own name written on them. It is to Philadelphia that Jesus speaks about "the hour of trial that is coming on the whole world to test the inhabitants of the earth." Spiritual faithfulness is not a game; it is about life and death.

(vii) The Final Letter Is for the Church in *Laodicea* (3:14–22).

The people of the church in Laodicea are reminded first of all that Jesus is "the faithful and true witness" and "the origin of God's creation" (cf. Col 1:15–20). This is God's world; he is its sovereign Lord. Jesus has authority over all creation. And, as John made clear to all the churches, God's people are to be "a kingdom of God's priests," serving God, and in God's name serving the whole earth and its inhabitants. How majestic a human vocation this is! And yet Laodicea, prosperous, well-heeled, self-sufficient, self-satisfied Laodicea, has lost its zeal, and has become a sickly, lukewarm group without either the heat of fire or the shock of cold. There were some hot springs in the area which were good for healing, and lower down in the valley some cold springs—good for refreshment in hot weather. But your lukewarm water is good for neither. If you try to drink it, you will want to spit it out! So in your spiritual life, you have become good for nothing. You have effectively shut Jesus out of his home, and he knocks for reentry. He wants to be with us, eating with us, having fellowship with us, allowing us to share in God's costly victory. But instead you do not realize that you are wretched, pitiable, poor, blind, naked. Open the door again to Christ and receive his gold in place of your worldly wealth, his white robe in place of your old clothes, his healing touch instead of your home-grown Laodicean remedies. Those who *conquer* have a right to sit with Jesus on his throne.

While the messages to each of the churches carry immediate relevance to many of today's Christian assemblies, the word against the complacency at Laodicea, a church which is reminded that Jesus is King of creation, is particularly pertinent to today's church at a time when together the human race is actively destroying much of God's good creation. Our assumed capacities for management and control and our self-centered consumerism are leading instead to death and destruction. The calling is for repentance, and change, and to welcome again the Risen Christ amongst us.

In summary, the Risen Jesus is walking among the churches, he who holds the seven stars, is the first and the last, speaks the word of truth with a sharp two-edged sword, his eyes like fire, his feet like bronze. He holds the seven spirits and the keys of David—presumably the keys to the New Jerusalem. He is the faithful and true witness, the beginning of God's creation. We recall what John said at the beginning: "I, John, your brother who share with you in Jesus, the persecution and the kingdom and the patient endurance" (1:9). We find the themes of "persecution, God's kingdom, and the call for patient endurance" recurring throughout the Book of Revelation. You may face persecution; Jesus Christ is King and in him the kingdom of God has decisively broken into our world; you are called to patient endurance (that is, faithful obedience), continuing with Christ in his ongoing loving engagement with this suffering world, for he is Lord.

We are made aware of the tensions between Christians and some claiming to be Jews, but who were probably Roman collaborators, in Smyrna and Philadelphia, but the real test is the extent to which the Christian churches have accommodated themselves to the culture of Empire, for example, the Nicolaitans in Ephesus and Pergamum. We are going to discover much more about the seductions of Empire (Rome, which John calls "Babylon") later in the

Book of Revelation. But in these seven letters the message is clear: if you are going to retain your discipleship and live faithfully and humanly when the allurements of Empire are all around you, be on your guard, and be prepared for persecution and suffering. Be especially aware of the ease with which you lose sight of your love for Christ through the temptations to fit in with the godless culture around you. Complacency and self-satisfaction are enemies of the faith. So, in all your tribulation, do not lose your love, keep faithful, do not be seduced by ungodly powers, nor play around in your spiritual life. Jesus Christ loves you. Jesus Christ has suffered for you and suffers with you. Wake up from your lack of diligence. Christ is the King! The decisive victory over all that is evil was won on the cross. Keep on patiently holding on in faith and endurance, and open the door again to Christ, the sovereign Lord of history and of all creation, the risen Lord of the church.

And the reason is that you have work to do. You are called to bear witness to Jesus Christ, and that will involve you in sharing in the war that Christ, through the power of his death and resurrection, is waging against evil with his weapons of self-giving love. The war is specifically against the agents of the Dragon—the Beast and the False Prophet whom we will meet in a later chapter. Christians who *conquer*—who are faithful even to the point of death if necessary—will be part of God's purpose to bring the nations of the earth and their rulers to repentance and to faith in Christ. God's purpose is not for individual Christians alone, nor indeed for the church alone, but for the whole of creation with its civilizations and cultures, its nations and skills—all the kingdom of this world is to become the kingdom of God. This is all part of what John means by "to conquer," namely to keep on resisting the allurements of Empire and stay faithful to Christ the Lamb, even if it means suffering. It is your behavior, living out your faith, not what you say you believe, that ultimately shows where you stand.

For some who read this, there is reassurance: to the one who conquers, there is blessing from God—protection from death, the blessing of a white stone with a new name on it, the morning star, white robes to wear, an honored place in God's temple, and a place with Jesus on his throne. Keep the faith! Do not lose heart! To other readers, these messages reveal uncomfortable truths: if you are a follower of Christ, you will need to change your ways.

That is always the way when the Risen Christ walks among the churches: giving reassurance and blessing, but also exposing what requires repentance and change. All through the Book of Revelation, we are faced with a separation and a choice. Will our allegiance be to the Empire with its attractions and yet its ultimate destructiveness? Or will it be to Jesus Christ as Lord and King?

The question for Ephesus is also the question for Eastbourne and Evanston; for Sanderstead and Seattle as well as Sardis; for Providence and Portland and Perth as well as Pergamum. How are we going to live Christianly—live humanly—in a social context that has abandoned God? How are we to stay faithful in our commitment to Christ when there are so many pressures from the secular world around us to fit in with their ways? We find ourselves too often at the mercy of what has been called "Mammon's kingdom." We have lost the sense which earlier generations maintained that history is something to do with the outworking of God's purposes, even of God's judgments. Today we are constantly faced with anti-creation pressures caused by human actions on our natural environment. Where is now the sense that "the earth is the Lord's"? Even in contemporary politics, we are sometimes made aware that there are "dark forces" at work. We can also understand something of the sense of alienation and injustice felt by many, including Christian brothers and sisters, who live under oppressive and totalitarian regimes where persecution, abuse, and even torture and death become political tools.

The strange Book of Revelation was written in the context of an oppressive empire, and some of the questions which we find ourselves asking were addressed in that very different context by the visions given to John on Patmos. The Risen Jesus still walks as Lord of the church among the candlesticks of all our local assemblies.

"Let anyone who has an ear listen to what the Spirit is saying to the churches."

The Risen Jesus Is Lord of the Church

The Church's one foundation
Is Jesus Christ her Lord;
She is His new creation
By water and the Word:
From heaven He came and sought her
To be his holy Bride,
With his own blood he bought her,
And for her life He died.

Elect from every nation
Yet one o'er all the earth,
Her charter of salvation
One Lord, one faith, one birth;
One holy name she blesses,
Partakes one holy food,
And to one hope she presses
With every grace endued.

Though with a scornful wonder
Men see her sore oppressed,
By schisms rent asunder,
By heresies distressed,
Yet saints their watch are keeping,
Their cry goes up, "How long?"
And soon the night of weeping
Shall be the morn of song.

'Mid toil and tribulation,
and tumult of her war,
She waits the consummation
Of peace for evermore;
Till with the vision glorious
Her longing eyes are blest,
And the great Church victorious
Shall be the Church at rest.

The Apocalypse of Jesus Christ

Yet she on earth hath union
With God the Three in One,
And mystic sweet communion
With those whose rest is won!
O happy ones and holy!
Lord give us grace that we,
Like them, the meek and lowly,
On high may dwell with Thee.

Samuel John Stone (1839–1900)

For Prayer, Reflection, Discussion

Reflect on John's description of Jesus:

> The faithful witness, the first born of the dead, the ruler
> of the kings of the earth . . . who loves us, and freed us
> from our sins by his blood, and made us to be a kingdom,
> priests serving his God and Father. (Rev 1:5–6)

The Risen Jesus is "in the midst" of your local Christian assembly / your church. He says, "I know your works."

What does he find to praise? Does he call you back to your first love? Does he strengthen your commitment and your resolve? Are there grounds for rebuke? In what ways is your church most likely to be tempted to follow the allurements of contemporary secular culture?

"Listen to what the Spirit is saying to the churches."

2

The Crucified Lamb Is the Lord of History

(Rev 4:1—8:5)

1. A Door Standing Open in Heaven

FROM A CHRISTIAN POINT of view, Revelation chapters 4 and 5 are two of the most thrilling and exciting chapters in the whole Bible, opening up for us, as they do, the worship which the whole of creation is offering to God. John, on the Island of Patmos, recording his vision from the risen Jesus and his commission to write what he sees, now says that "in the Spirit" he sees heaven's door standing open. "Heaven," we remind ourselves, is part of God's creation: that part which is God's sphere of being with all his angels, usually hidden from view in our sphere of being on earth. But John the prophet can now see through heaven's open door. He sees a sort of throne room, a sort of temple, a sort of law court; what metaphor can he use to describe the majesty of God? Now in his vision he sees some meaning to the struggles and sufferings which he and his fellow Christians are having to cope with in the face of possible coming persecution—even martyrdom—from the oppressive and seductive Roman Empire. Part of the vision is past: a Lamb who has been slain; part is future: the judgments of God which are to come. All merge into his present vision of God, seated on the throne with a jeweled robe in omnipotent majesty, and with a rainbow like a halo round the throne. Here is a different perspective, a "perspective from heaven," if we may use the phrase, "God's point of view," on all the politics and trials and struggles which are taking place on earth.

The rainbow is a clear reminder of God's covenant with Noah and with every living creature. It is God's "Yes!" to the whole of creation. In the story of the flood, Noah gets out of the ark, kneels down in the mud, and prays. And God says to him:

> "This is the sign of the covenant that I make between me and you and every living creature that is with you, for all future generations. I have set my bow in the clouds, and it shall be a sign of the covenant between me and the earth." (Gen 9:12–13)

The flood had been a sign of God's condemnation of all that was evil in the world. The rainbow was a sign of God's mercy in the storm. Here is a vivid illustration of the truth about God, expressed so beautifully much later in the Wisdom book Sirach: "Equal to his majesty is his mercy" (Sir 2:18). John sees this truth in his vision through heaven's door: the history of God's dealings with his people, from the story of the covenant with Noah onwards, is the account of God's majesty inextricably linked with God's mercy. The symbols of the great power of God the Creator which John now sees in the throne room, are surrounded by the rainbow, a wonderful sign of God's compassion and mercy. All the turbulence, flood, and storm of the world of idolatrous Empire and of Christians' tribulation is held within the majesty and mercy of God.

Then John sees round the throne twenty-four elders, dressed in the white robes of victory, symbolizing their union with Christ. They represent all God's faithful people—perhaps twelve for the tribes of Israel and then twelve for the apostles of Jesus. Some of the imagery would be recognizable for those who knew of the court of Imperial Rome. Here it is made clear that whatever Imperial Rome aspires to be, it is God who is Lord of history. The whole of the history of God's people is represented by the twenty-four elders. Jesus is himself later described as carrying the name of

"King of kings and Lord of lords" (19:16). From the throne John sees reminders (lightning and thunder) of what happened in that crucial time in the history of God's people, when Moses received God's holy word, the Torah, on Mount Sinai (Exod 19:16). John sees in front of the throne "the seven spirits of God"—a phrase which usually refers to the Holy Spirit. Here is God, the sovereign Creator, ruling through Word and Spirit, sovereign over the history of the world. And in front of the throne "there was something like a sea of glass." It is not quite clear what this means. Is it to give some distance between the throne and John who is looking in—a reminder of God's great holiness? Or are we to recall that vision of God's throne in the Book of Daniel when the sea was being blown by a huge tempest? There and elsewhere in the Old Testament, the sea stands for danger, chaos, disorder. Remember the Leviathan, sometimes thought of as the sea monster whom the psalmist regards as an enemy of God (e.g., Ps 74:14), although elsewhere even the monster is portrayed as a creature of God and the sea recognized as part of God's creation (Ps 104:25, 26). Recall also the time of Jesus, when the storm blew up on the sea of Galilee and Jesus commanded the wind to cease and there was a great calm. Maybe that is the picture here. In heaven, the sea looks calm, like glass, like crystal: a picture, perhaps, that what is still turbulent on earth is now stilled before the throne of God? John will later describe "the sea" of turbulent humanity on earth (17:15) from which the Beast arises to cause havoc among God's people. The sea on earth in John's vision is often a sign of chaos and disorder both in creation and in humanity. Here in chapter 4, however, the heavenly counterpart to "the sea" is still and calm. And we are told at the very end of the book that in the new heaven and the new earth, "there was no more sea" (22:1).

2. Four Living Creatures

John's spiritual vision develops as he looks through heaven's door, and he sees four living creatures, representatives of the whole of creation: the majestic lion, the powerful ox, the soaring eagle, and the human being. The images are very close to the four creatures in Ezekiel's vision (Ezek 1:1–14). Indeed, much else in this chapter has resonance with visions in Ezekiel. Much has been made of the significance of the four creatures. As early as the second century, the theologian Irenaeus interpreted them to refer to different aspects of Christ's ministry: the lion, he suggested, portrayed Christ's leadership and royal power; the calf (ox) signified his sacrifice; the "face of a man" spoke of Christ's incarnation; and the flying eagle pointed to the gift of the Spirit hovering over the church.[1] Irenaeus then connected each creature with one of the four Gospels, and other theologians followed him (though not always making quite the same connections). In the Book of Revelation we do indeed find many references to royal power, exercised through the sacrificial service of the incarnate Lord in the power of the Spirit. All that is true, but I think the primary point for us to take from the vision of four living creatures round the throne is that they represent all aspects of God's good creation. The creation narrative of Genesis 1 includes the birds, the wild animals, the cattle, humankind. And the psalmist calls "wild animals and all cattle, creeping things and flying birds, kings of the earth and all people" to "praise the name of the Lord" (Ps 148:1–11). All creation is here.

This entire world is God's world, and it is fundamentally good. "God saw everything that he had made, and indeed it was very good" (Gen 1:31). Creation, we shall discover all too soon, has been infected with evil things, and distorted out of its good patterns and life-giving resources. But the picture in Revelation 4 is of all God's creatures including humanity worshiping before God's throne. "Day and night without ceasing they sing 'Holy, holy, holy, the Lord God Almighty, who was, and is and is to come'" (4:8). The whole of creation is depicted worshiping God the Creator. The twenty-four elders take off their own crowns and cast them humbly before God's throne, in recognition of God's honor and glory and power: "You are worthy, our Lord and God, to receive glory and honor and power, for you created all things, and by your will they were created and have their being" (4:11) "By your will":

---

1. Irenaeus, *Against Heresies*, III.11.8.

the whole of creation exists by the will of God. The will of God, disclosed in Jesus to be shaped by love, is the ultimate power in this universe. God is Lord of creation and Lord of history. That is ultimately a reassuring thought for a suffering church, confronted by the violent and coercive powers of Empire, and the unexplained suffering throughout creation, although, as we constantly discover, no one is exempt from the violence and suffering of the world.

The angel says (4:1) that he will show John "what must take place after this"—that is, the story of human destiny, the eternal plan of God, the war of God against evil, the liberating judgments, the fulfillment of the ultimate victory of Christ. All that follows has to be set in this context: the whole of God's good creation, which John Calvin called "the theatre"[2] of God's glory, is called to the worship of God the Creator. God has not abandoned the creation—it is all still a central part of God's purpose. All the other powers that wage war against God have to be set against this: true power lies with the Lord, the holy one, the Creator, God Almighty. Evil may be very real, and there are tasks for God's people to do to rescue God's earth from the evil that is embedded in it, but God's purposes will be vindicated. There can be hope in the faithfulness of God.

3. The Crucified Lamb

When we turn over to Revelation chapter 5, we discover that we are in the presence not only of God the Almighty Father who is Creator, but also of the Lamb of God, who is Redeemer, through whom all things are made new, and of the seven flaming torches, "which are the seven spirits of God"—in other words, of God the Holy Spirit. Creation and Redemption are all part of the work of God the Holy Trinity: Creator, Redeemer, and Holy Spirit, the Giver of Life.

In God's right hand John sees that there is a scroll with seven seals. We are getting used to "seven." We have heard of seven messages to seven churches. There are seven seals in this part of the

2. Calvin, *Institutes*, I.vi.2.

Book of Revelation. The next section brings us seven trumpets. Later, there are seven bowls of God's wrath against evil and seven last plagues to afflict the earth. Each section opens us up to the judgments of God, points to God's deliverance from evil, and restrains the power of evil from hurting God's people. It seems as though John is going around in cycles of sevens, each telling us from different perspectives about God's world, about the powers of evil, and about the judgments of God. And in each cycle, in different ways, Jesus is establishing God's kingdom on earth. God's scroll seems to be the book of this world's history and destiny, and it is sealed with seven seals. A smaller, earth-sized scroll appears in Revelation chapter 10. Probably this is this same scroll which here we see in heaven, but smaller, earth-sized, and there put into the hands of John the prophet. There it is described as containing "the mystery of God"—presumably God's plan of salvation for humanity and creation, a history now coming to its fulfillment. Until now it is God's secret—God has limited his own power in this way. From the stories of early Genesis onwards, the Bible makes clear that the fulfillment of our history and the destiny of God's world are to be achieved through obedient human beings. That was the plan depicted in the garden of Eden: humanity in God's image is given responsibility to cultivate and protect God's garden. Some Christians have wrongly understood that phrase in Genesis 2, alongside the reference to "dominion" in Genesis chapter 1 to mean that, as Descartes put it, "we are masters and possessors of nature."[3] Christians influenced by such views have assumed that they authorize us humans with the right and the freedom to extract from and make use of the resources of God's earth without regard to caring and protecting God's garden. Francis Bacon was much nearer the spirit of Genesis 2 when he wrote, "Man is but the servant and interpreter of nature."[4]

So God's intention from Eden onwards was to achieve God's purposes through the obedience of human beings, and in their service of God's creation. It lies behind God's covenant with Abraham

3. Descartes, *Method*, 78.
4. Bacon, *Instauration*, 31.

and so into the history of Israel. God's purposes are often to be fulfilled through human agencies. All creation has been waiting for a
human being who is worthy to put God's purposes for the whole
of creation into effect. In the imagery of John's vision in Revelation chapter 5, creation has been waiting for someone to open the
seals on God's book. The question is not "who is strong enough to
open the seals?" nor "who is clever enough?" but "who is *worthy*
to unlock God's secrets?" And then, as John weeps because he does
not know the answer, one of the elders tells him that the "Lion
of the tribe of Judah," a phrase used by some Hebrew writers to
indicate God's messiah, the "Root of David," that is in the royal
line of Israel's great king, "has conquered," so that he is worthy to
unlock God's secrets.

So John looks up expecting to see a Lion: symbol of God's
majesty and power. Instead—and we need to catch the anticlimax
of this!—he sees a Lamb, standing as if it had been slaughtered.
The Lamb as well as the Lion are both images applied to Jesus,
God's Messiah, the Redeemer. The Lion is less prominent in the
Book of Revelation from now on, but we are going to meet the
Lamb quite a lot. Why "Lamb"? There are so many references to
God's provision of a "lamb" in the Hebrew Bible that it is hard to
know what may have been most in mind here. Perhaps it was the
story of Abraham and Isaac, with father and son together on the
mountain, when God provides an unexpected lamb for the sacrifice. That was a lamb of God's gracious provision. Most likely the
Revelation reference is to Passover-night before the exodus from
Egypt, when the Passover lamb was a sign of God's liberation, as
the people sheltered in the place marked by the blood of the lamb.
Maybe it was the lamb of sacrifice in the Book of Leviticus, which
kept alive in the minds of the people God's promises of grace and
forgiveness. Maybe it was the Suffering Servant in the book of Isaiah, led as "a lamb to the slaughter . . . by whose stripes we have
been healed." All these are different aspects throughout the history
of God's people of the work of Christ the Redeemer: God's unexpected provision, God's liberation, God's forgiveness, and God's

suffering love. It is the crucified Lamb of God who is worthy to open the seals of God's scroll of world history.

Another image sometimes also used of the messiah is of the great horned ram who leads the sheep to their victory. The Lamb in Revelation chapter 5 has *seven* horns ("seven" stands for completeness, perfection). Seven horns: the perfect leader! And the Lamb has seven eyes suggesting a perfect seeing and knowing of all things: the risen Christ knowingly present as the Holy Spirit throughout God's creation. A "horned" Lamb means a powerful Lamb. The Lamb who was slain is also the Lion. The Lion is a Lamb. The majestic power of the Lion is the power of the peaceable, self-giving, sacrificial love of the Lamb. In Christ, the vulnerable Lamb, God's majestic power and compassionate mercy belong together. What a contrast to the power we shall discover is characteristic of the empire: violence, coercion, and Death.

When the Lamb had taken the scroll, the twenty-four elders and the four living creatures round God's throne sang a new song. We will discover many things throughout the Book of Revelation described as "new" (new name, New Jerusalem, new heaven, new earth, God "makes all things new," 21:5). Here the company of heaven sing a new song—to celebrate the victory of the Lamb: "for you were slaughtered, and by your blood you ransomed for God saints from every tribe and language and people and nation" (5:9). Through the shed blood of the Lamb, God's people throughout their history have found grace, liberation, forgiveness, victory. But more than that: God's people have been given a destiny and a task—"you have made them a kingdom of priests serving our God and they will reign on earth" (5:10).

We met that phrase "kingdom of priests" before. It comes several times in the Book of Revelation, and it recalls the word in Exodus that God's people should be kings and priests (Exod 19: 6). Both "king" and "priest" are words used of God's messiah, and John's vision now, as in so many places, picks up Old Testament images, applies them to Jesus, and makes of them something new. John is realizing that God's purpose is for human beings, living in obedience to God's will, to share in Christ's kingly rule over the earth and his priestly ministry before God. This is our ultimate destiny. There will be sufferings and deaths, even martyrdoms on the way, as God works to rid the world of the evils that have devastated and disfigured the whole creation. John later speaks of God "destroying those who destroy the earth" (11:18). But throughout history, God is creating a new community (later called "New Jerusalem") of new people, to share life with him in a new world, a new heaven, and a new earth, in the victorious kingdom of Christ's glory.

Chapter 5 ends with the whole of creation caught up in a hymn of praise. If we listen carefully, we can almost hear Handel's music playing:

> "Worthy is the Lamb that was slaughtered
> to receive power and wealth and wisdom and might
> and honor and glory and blessing . . .
> To the one seated on the throne and to the Lamb
> be blessing and honor and glory and might
> forever and ever!"
> And the four living creatures said "Amen!" and the elders fell
> down and worshiped. (5:12–14)

4. The Lamb Opens the Scroll with Seven Seals

The Lamb now starts to open the seals on God's book: the first four, then five and six, and then there is an interlude before the last, seventh seal. In John's vision, the risen Jesus is unveiling God's secrets about the world's history and destiny—and actually setting in train the whole process of divine judgment, with all its horrors, before we come towards the end of the Book of Revelation to the climax of all history: God's victory over all that is evil, the coming kingdom of Christ's glory and peace—the coming "Day of the Lord." We discover that the scroll of world history and destiny opens up the story of world judgment and world liberation.

We need to pause on the word "judgment" because it has often come to mean almost exclusively "condemnation." And indeed, judgment does often lead to condemnation and punishment. In the Old Testament, there is often a sense that people's sins bring their own judgment on themselves. (The psalmist, for example, extols "God, the righteous judge," but goes on to speak of those who do not repent; they "make a pit, digging it out, and fall into the hole that they have made. Their mischief returns upon their own heads, and on their own heads their violence descends," Ps 7:11, 15–16) But the word "judgment" is also used more neutrally to mean "discern, give a verdict, distinguish, diagnose, bring choices to light, decide." So, the psalmist prays: "Give the king your justice, O God . . . may he judge your people with righteousness, and your poor with justice" (Ps 72:1–4). Part of a doctor's judgment, for example, is to distinguish the good and the healthy from the evil and the malignant. One aspect of judgment is purifying the infected parts and liberating new life, while another is condemnation and the destruction of what is caught up in evil.

5. The First Four Seals (6:1–8)

The opening of the first four seals set free four horsemen to ride about the earth and create havoc. John in the vision is summoned to see, and he hears the four living creatures calling out the riders on their horses. He is being invited to understand—from God's perspective, so to speak—what is actually going on in the world. In this vivid imagery, the horsemen are major forces in world history; they are agents of Empire, but always held back by the sovereign power of God. The horsemen represent evils and tribulations never willed by God, though always restrained by God. God's little frightened church must hold on to this fact: the destructive forces of evil in the world can only exercise the power that God allows, even though it already seems—even at this early stage in the life of the church, as some of the letters to the seven churches illustrate—that compromise with Empire was becoming too frequent. Sadly, we can recognize these horsemen only too well in our world today; they represent for us, too, some of the effects of Empire: oppressive, often violent totalitarian rule.

The first horseman on a white horse represents conquest. He has a bow and rides out to conquer. The second carrying a sword rides on a red horse, signifying local disputes and battles, social disorder, perhaps bloody civil war. The third horseman on a black horse carries scales to measure and ration food. He illustrates economic injustice: the bread for the poor will be scarce, even though the luxuries for the rich (oil and wine) will still be available. Injustices in food resources lead to famine. The fourth, on a pale green horse, represents pestilence and Death and Hades. These horsemen describe the Roman Empire when John was writing: conquest, war, famine, the power of Death. They are also the effects of God's judgments on Israel's sinful ways described by the prophet Ezekiel: "they shall fall by the sword, by famine, by pestilence" (Ezek 6:11). John's vision seems to bring together a picture of idolatrous power and human suffering, under the judgment of God, the lord of history.

Perhaps John also had in mind the words of Jesus in the Gospels:

> "When you hear of wars and rumors of wars, do not be alarmed; this must take place, but the end is not yet. Nation will rise against nation, and kingdom against kingdom; there will be earthquakes in various places; there will be famines. This is but the beginning of the birth-pangs." (Mark 13:7–8)

The tribulation the churches face is the "birth pangs" of God's new world waiting to be born. In John's Gospel, Jesus says to his followers, "In the world you will have tribulation but take courage! I have conquered the world" (John 16:33). These four horsemen in Revelation chapter 6 describe much of our world today: conquest, civil war, economic injustice, and death and pestilence. We saw them in the Gulags of Stalin's state socialism; we saw them in Nazi Germany; and they are alive and well today in the global forces that are destructive of human life and well-being. At a much more local and minor level, we have seen some of their hoofprints in the UK Brexit debates following the 2016 Referendum about whether the United Kingdom should leave the European Union. "Leave" and "Remain" campaigns quickly became, for some protagonists, all-consuming ideologies bent on conquest. The other sides were called "traitors," "enemies of the people," "collaborators." All that mattered was winning. There was social disorder; there was economic injustice. There was much "hate speech," and there were death threats for opposing members of Parliament—even one terrible murder. The horsemen are not Hollywood-type symbols of the end of the world; they are violent powers at work throughout human history and in different ways even today.

There are strong echoes of those hoofbeats in an article by George Monbiot in *The Guardian* in April 2019. He is arguing about the failure of the modern capitalist system, arising, he says, from several factors, including the assumption of perpetual growth.

> Capitalism collapses without growth, yet perpetual growth on a finite planet leads inexorably to environmental calamity . . . The threatened collapse of our life-support systems is bigger by far than [notice!] war, famine, pestilence or economic crisis, though it is likely to incorporate all four.[5]

In Revelation chapter 6, John is still looking through the open door into heaven. He realizes that God knows about all these horsemen and their destructive powers; John understands that God decrees that the idolatrous powers of Empire need to be restrained and their evil destroyed, and the suffering they cause put right. John has seen the opening of the first four seals, and now he looks to see what happens when the fifth seal is opened.

6. The Fifth Seal (6:9–11)

Opening seal number five brings John's focus back to the throne room of heaven, and to the altar. And there under the altar are some of the victims of these evil horsemen—those who had been martyred for their faith in Jesus. In the Book of Leviticus, the phrase "under the altar" refers to the place of sacrifice. Perhaps here, the martyrs, who in their own way have shared in the sacrifice and sufferings of Christ, find their place under God's altar.

5. Monbiot, "Declare Capitalism Dead."

This is God's recognition of their self-giving, and perhaps provides a place of protection. It seems that the deaths of the suffering martyrs are somehow used by God to bring about victory over evil. The martyrs wear the white robes of victory. They are crying out to God, "Sovereign Lord, how long before you judge this evil and vindicate us who have suffered?" The text rather brutally says: "How long until you avenge our blood?" (6:10). Although it feels like a prayer for vengeance, it is in fact a prayer for justice from God to vindicate those who have been so cruelly abused. The phrase "the inhabitants of earth" which John uses here and elsewhere, does not mean "everyone," but refers to the ungodly world (rather as we use "the world" in the phrase "the world, the flesh and the devil" to refer to "wordliness" as opposed to "godliness"). The important thing for John to discover is that the prayers and cries and sufferings of the victims of oppression are heard right in the heart of heaven. That is good news, especially for those parts of our world today where human beings face oppression and sometimes persecution and are the innocent victims of violence.

7. The Sixth Seal (6:12–17)

Now the sixth seal is opened, and John has a vision of a cosmic catastrophe in which spiritual powers seem to be shaking the earth. God's anger is released against everything throughout human history that has ruined God's creation. We read of earthquakes, sky falling, mountains moving—with quotations from Joel and Isaiah. These are often the prophetic signs of the coming of the Day of the Lord. They appear several times in John's vision, as again and again we are led through various seals, trumpets, and bowls of wrath towards the coming Day of God. The coming Day of God is often described as a Day of Liberation. It is also a day of God's "wrath" against evil. John's vision is also about the downfall of "the kings of the earth" and magnates and generals and the rich and powerful. The list in fact includes "everyone, slave and free," and also the great global powers and institutions which throughout history imprison and enslave people. We pause again on the phrase "the kings of the earth." It means those human rulers who claim power without reference to God. The "kings of the earth" are going to find themselves in conflict with the King of kings. In the very first chapter of Revelation, it was said of the Risen Jesus that he is "the faithful witness, the first born from the dead, the ruler of the kings of the earth" (1:5). In the sixth seal the "kings" are depicted as cowering in terror in anticipation of God's judgment and what will follow it. In this vision, proud rulers of earth who do not acknowledge the majesty of God find themselves looking for caves in which to hide when face to face with the victorious Crucified Lamb of God.

Once again, we think of Jesus' words in the Gospels:

> "Immediately after the suffering of those days, the sun will be darkened, and the moon will not give its light; the stars will fall from heaven, and the powers of heaven will be shaken. Then the sign of the Son of Man will appear in heaven, and then all the tribes of the earth will mourn." (Matt 24:29–30)

In a shocking phrase in Rev 6:16, we read of "the wrath of the Lamb," where "wrath," about which we shall hear much more later on, describes the reaction of a righteous God against all evil and injustice, a reaction which stems from God's love for suffering people. "God's wrath" is the working out in world history of the consequences of human rejection of God and God's will. It is the wrath of sacrificial love from which "nothing can separate us." It is a wrath that liberates. Again and again throughout the Book of Revelation there are echoes of the story of the liberation of God's people from the enslaving power of Pharaoh in Egypt, so that they can find a new life as God's people in a new land. And so here where we read of God's judgment and wrath, we also read of the victorious Passover Lamb. The whole weight of God's condemnation of evil was carried by the Lamb of God on Calvary; his Resurrection opened a new day, the first fruits of a new creation. We, and all God's church, in Ephesus or Sardis; in Europe or the USA, are living in the light of Christ's death and resurrection and are awaiting the ultimate disclosure of his kingly rule. That will be the Day of the Lord's Coming, throughout the whole of creation and the whole of history, when all the terrors caused by the horsemen and the evils perpetrated by the kings of the earth are eventually brought to nothing. Now is still a time of tribulation and of waiting. But the Lamb is now the Lord of history, the "ruler of the kings of the earth." He is history's "Beginning and End" (21:6; 22:13)— its source and its goal. Indeed, he is its center and its meaning, summing up in himself all that world history and the whole of creation signify in the purposes of God.

The good news, which develops through the book, is that although "the kings of the earth" and their nations here cower before the wrath of the Lamb, there will be people "from every nation and tribe and people and language" who stand before the throne and in front of the Lamb, singing of salvation (7:10). It is John and indeed the whole church who are called to "prophesy" and preach the eternal gospel to "peoples and nations, languages and kings" (10:11). Even in the earthquake which signifies the coming Day of Wrath, there were many—notice! "many"—who were saved and "gave glory to God" (11:13). Later we also read how the redeemed of God sing: "All nations will come before you, for your righteous acts have been revealed" (15:4). In the war which the forces of evil wage against the Lamb, "the Lamb will overcome them because he is Lord of lords and King of kings" (17:14). And most wonderfully, in the new heaven and the new earth, the "kings of the earth" appear again in John's vision to acknowledge God's majesty, and there they bring their splendor and their glory, and the honor of the nations, right into the holy city of God. The leaves of the tree of life are for the "healing of the nations" (22:2), and the nations— now redeemed and healed—walk by the light of the Lamb (21:24). Jesus is indeed Lord of history, the ruler of the kings of the earth.

So much of John's vision has resonance with the psalms, among them this from Psalm 2:

> Why do the nations conspire,
> and the peoples plot in vain?
> The kings of the earth set themselves,
> and the rules take counsel together
> against the Lord, and his anointed, saying,

"Let us burst their bonds asunder,
and cast their cords from us."

He who sits in the heavens laughs;
the Lord has them in derision.
Then he will speak to them in his wrath,
and terrify them in his fury, saying,
"I have set my king on Zion, my holy hill."

I will tell of the decree of the Lord:
He said to me, "You are my Son;
today I have begotten you.
Ask of me and I will make the nations your heritage,
and the ends of the earth your possession.
You shall break them with a rod of iron,
and dash them in pieces like a potter's vessel."

Now therefore, O kings, be wise;
be warned, O rulers of the earth.
Serve the Lord with fear,
and with trembling kiss his feet,
or he will be angry, and you will perish in the way;
for his wrath is quickly kindled.
Happy are all who take refuge in him. .

To return now to Revelation chapter 6: opening the sixth seal
has brought us to the beginning of a vision of the coming Day of
the Lord. There is terror around the godless earth. Kings and the
rich and powerful, and slaves and free, are hiding from the search-
ing presence of the Lamb. Then the prophet quite understandably
asks, "Who can stand?" (6:17).

8. A Breathing Space

Then there is an interlude, a reassuring reminder to God's suffering churches that the followers of Christ have no need to fear the
tumult around them: they are safe in God's care even in the Day
of the Wrath of the Lamb. So chapter 7 begins with angels holding
back destructive winds so that they cannot damage God's people.

Destructive winds will come, there is still suffering ahead, but first, God is going to protect you with his own mark of security on your forehead. All God's people, from all the tribes and all the nations, are safe. All God's people are sealed with God's security mark, and all are joining in creation's praise. John surely remembers God's promise, made so long ago to Abraham, that through him all the families of the earth would be blessed. God's people hear the angel's reassurance in this view of God's world as its painful history is drawn into the Day of God's future of justice, healing and redemption. And now in John's vision, all the images become conflated, though not contrasted: the Lamb, who is the Lion, becomes also the Shepherd. Tucked into the middle of the strong themes in the Book of Revelation calling the ungodly to repentance and enlisting followers of the Lamb to engage in conflict with the evil forces of Empire, we find this gentle but powerful word to encourage the suffering church:

> They will hunger no more and thirst no more . . . the Lamb at the center of the throne will be their Shepherd, and he will guide them to springs of the water of life, and God will wipe away every tear from their eyes. (7:15–17)

Even though the destructive winds still blow, you who belong to Christ are sealed and protected under God's special care. "In the world you will have tribulation; take courage! I have overcome the world!" (John 16:33).

9. The Seventh Seal (8:1–5)

At long last, we come to the seventh and final seal. We have had horsemen bringing conquest and war, famine and deadly pestilence. We have heard from the martyrs who have died for their faith calling, "How long, O Lord?" We have experienced the signs of the end-time; warnings about the coming Day of the Lord; terror before the wrath of the Lamb, and yet the protected security of God's people. John's vision is drawing us towards the climax of the Day of the Lord.

So, the seventh seal is opened. And, astonishingly, all falls silent.

There is something even more important for John still to learn about the suffering, persecuted church. He has to learn of the power of the church's prayers. God is apparently calling all creation to be silent, so that now the one focus can be on the prayers of God's people. So John sees an angel take their prayers and mix them with incense in a golden censer and offer it to God. Then, remarkably, the prayers of God's people are mixed with fire from God's altar—fire to destroy and fire to purify—and thrown down on the earth. We may remember the text in Luke where Jesus says that he came "to send fire onto the earth" (Luke 12:49). John experiences peals of thunder, rumblings, flashes of lightning, and an earthquake; once again, all signs of God's Coming Day. So is this going to be part of the power of God's victory over evil—the prayers of God's people mixed with the fire from God's altar?

The Scottish theologian T. F. Torrance once wrote:

> As the seventh seal is opened, we read the profounder mysteries of world events. What are the real master-powers behind the world, and what are the deeper secrets of our destiny? Here is the astounding answer: the prayers of the saints and the fire of God. More potent than all the dark and mighty powers let loose in the world, and more powerful than anything else, is the power of prayer set ablaze by the fire of God and cast upon the earth.[6]

Torrance is saying that the prayers of God's people can have an explosive effect on world history. Could it be that empires fall because God joins his fire with the prayers of powerless people who keep on praying for God's kingdom to come? We often, no doubt, feel that our prayers have little effect, but the picture here is of the prayers of God's people becoming part of how God's kingdom comes. That is why Jesus taught us to pray specifically for the coming of God's kingdom.

Whatever the horsemen and the kings of the earth can do, God listens to and sets ablaze with his fire the prayers of his people.

6. Torrance, *Apocalypse Today*, 72–73.

The seventh seal now takes us, in the next chapters, from the throne room of heaven to terrible plagues let loose on earth by the sound of angelic trumpets. God's creation is in jeopardy. Yet the Lord of history is the King of all creation, and ultimately John will hear the angels' shout: "the kingdom of this world becomes the kingdom of our God and of his Christ" (11:15).

And the worship from four living creatures around the throne, the twenty-four elders, ten thousand times ten thousand angels, and "every creature in heaven and on earth and under the earth and on the sea" continues to be offered in praise of God Almighty and the Crucified Lamb.

The Crucified Lamb Is the Lord of History

Crown Him with many crowns, the Lamb upon his throne;
Hark! how the heavenly anthem drowns all music but its own:
Awake, my soul, and sing of Him who died for thee,
And hail Him as thy matchless King through all eternity.

Crown Him the Lord of life, who triumphed o'er the grave,
And rose victorious in the strife for those He came to save.
His glories now we sing, who died and rose on high,
Who died eternal life to bring, and lives that death may die.

Crown Him the Lord of love; Behold His hands and side.
Those wound yet visible above in beauty glorified:
No angel in the sky can fully bear that sight,
But downward bends his burning eye at mysteries so bright.

Crown Him the Lord of peace, whose power a scepter sways
from pole to pole, that wars may cease, and all be prayer and
praise.
His reign shall know no end. And round His pierced feet
Fair flowers of Paradise extend their fragrance ever sweet.

Crown Him the Lord of years, the Potentate of time.
Creator of the rolling spheres, ineffably sublime.
All hail, Redeemer, hail! For Thou hast died for me:
Thy praise shall never, never fail throughout eternity.

Matthew Bridges (1800–1894)

For Prayer, Reflection, Discussion

How does the imagery of the Lamb, and the Lion, inform your understanding of Jesus Christ?

Reflect on this scene of worship:

> When [the Lamb] had taken the scroll, the four living creatures and the twenty-four elders fell before the Lamb, each holding a harp and golden bowls full of incense, which are the prayers of the saints. They sing a new song:
>
>> "You are worthy to take the scroll and to open its seals, for you were slaughtered and by your blood you ransomed for God saints from every tribe and language and people and nations;
>> You have made them to be a kingdom and priests serving our God, and they will reign on earth . . .
>> "Worthy is the Lamb that was slaughtered to receive power and wealth and wisdom and might and honour and glory and blessing! . . .
>> "To the one seated on the throne and to the Lamb be blessing and honour and glory and might for ever and ever! Amen!" (Rev 5:8–10, 12, 13)]

Recall the martyrs whose witness cost them their lives. Their prayer "How long, O Lord?" (Rev 6:10) echoes several of the psalms, for example:

> How long, O Lord? Will you forget me forever?
> How long will you hide your face from me?
> How long must I bear pain in my soul,
> and have sorrow in my heart all day long?
> How long shall my enemy be exalted over me? (Ps 13:1–2)

Think about times when you have prayed this prayer, or when it might be right for you to pray this prayer.

Is it helpful to think of our prayers set ablaze by the fire of God? What do you think this means? What does it do to your understanding of prayer?

How should we pray for today's martyrs, the oppressed, the persecuted, victims of terror, survivors of childhood abuse?

3

Jesus Is King of All Creation

(Rev 8:6—11:19)

1. Seven Angels with Seven Trumpets

IN THIS OUR THIRD chapter, we learn how ultimately the kingdom of this world—beset, as we saw in our last chapter, by tribulations, conquest, wars, famines, and deadly pestilence—becomes the kingdom of our God and of his Christ. This section of Revelation ends with a song of triumph and victory, and with the glorious answer to the patient prayers of Christ's church: "Your kingdom come." This will be announced by the sound of a trumpet:

> Then the seventh angel blew his trumpet, and there were loud voices in heaven, saying,
> "The kingdom of this world has become the kingdom of our Lord and of his Christ,
> and he will reign for ever and ever."
> Then the twenty-four elders who sit on their thrones before God fell on their faces and worshiped God, singing,
> "We give you thanks, Lord God Almighty,
> who are and who were,
> for you have taken your great power
> and begun to reign.
> The nations raged,

> but your wrath has come,
> and the time for judging the dead,
> for rewarding your servants the prophets
> and saints and all who fear your name,
> both small and great,
> and for destroying those who destroy the earth." (11:15–18)

But before that seventh Last Trumpet sounds there are six earlier trumpets which sound with very different notes.

In the Hebrew Bible, before the giving of the Ten Commandments through Moses on Mount Sinai, a warning trumpet had sounded: God will speak! Sometimes trumpets announce judgment or warn the people or call them to repentance (cf. Jer 6:17; Ezek 33:2). Sometimes they celebrate a great deliverance. On occasion, as with the Last Trumpet here, they proclaim the enthronement of the king. But before we get to the Last Trumpet, there are horrible natural disasters and plagues to be coped with. And more than that, we discover that underneath all the sufferings that God's people are going through, there is a spiritual battle being fought. Beneath world powers there are supernatural powers, sometimes demonic powers of evil. Although we know that Christ has conquered all these powers on the cross, God still allows them limited effect in order to give time to bring a rebellious world back to God. The wrath of God is inseparable from the love of God. We can hear both love and judgment in the first four trumpets and their call to repentance.

Recall the pattern of the seven seals in our previous chapter. The scroll was opened by the Lamb of God. There were the first four seals of horsemen, then two more rather different seals, then an interlude when God's people received God's mark of protection in their tribulation, then finally, the seventh seal was opened, and we reached the pointers towards the coming Day of the Lord. That was the scroll of the world's history and destiny, holding the mystery of God's place of salvation and the vocation of God's church at a time of suffering and persecution.

This present section of the Book of Revelation follows a similar pattern with the seven trumpets. First, four trumpets, then two rather different trumpets, then an interlude when God's people are protected and given a commission, then with the Last Trumpet we reach pointers to the coming Day of the Lord, when God's kingly reign on earth becomes visible. As with the seven seals, this also is the story of the world's destiny and the vocation of God's church at a time of suffering and persecution, but now it is told from a different perspective. Now we are not so much thinking of conquests and wars and famine and pestilence, but of the *spiritual battles* that underlie them—especially the battle between the kingly rule of God and the evil demonic kingdom of worldliness with its tortures, terrors, and persecutions, which continually seeks to destroy God's good creation and God's holy people.

We remember that John, our author, has described himself as having been an exile on the island of Patmos, sharing with his brothers and sisters in Christ "the tribulation, the kingdom, the patient endurance." If our last section was mostly about the church's *tribulation*, this section leads to the victory of God, when the kingdom of the world becomes the *kingdom of God*. John's vision seems to move out of the throne room of heaven to see the work of Christ establishing the rule of heaven on earth. And much of the focus of these present chapters is on the earth—as God's creation, but an earth which is being devastated by powerful forces of destruction that are later called "the destroyers of the earth" (11:18), which are themselves ultimately destroyed.

2. The First Four Trumpets Release the Plagues (8:6–13)

We are now in Revelation chapter 8. After the purifying fire from the golden censer and the prayers of God's people set ablaze by the fire of God, the seven angels get ready to blow their trumpets. When the first four trumpets are sounded, plagues are released onto the earth. There is hail and fire, and the grass is burned up. A volcano on fire is cast into the sea. The sea itself becomes like blood, killing its living creatures. A poisonous star called Wormwood, a metaphor for bitterness, is polluting the waters. The sun, moon, and stars are darkened. The angels blow their trumpets and devastation hits all God's creation: the earth, the sea, the rivers, and the sky. In John's scary vision, *one-third* of the whole of God's earth is affected, and suffering is caused for people through the suffering of the earth. This is God's earth, and God is sovereign over it all, although God allows spiritual forces and natural forces to have their freedom. And they can function like trumpets awaking us to repent and change.

John may have had various natural events in mind. There was an eclipse of the sun in AD 68, when the sun was darkened, and the day was without light. And, of course, John might be thinking of the eruption of Vesuvius in AD 79, which was still very clear in people's memories, with its mountain on fire, its lava flow reaching the sea, its ash clouds, and its destruction of Pompeii and other nearby towns and settlements. John, in recording his vision, uses what were believed to be cosmic events to give him the language in which to speak of the spiritual forces which are at work in the world. He interprets these as trumpet calls from God: calls for repentance.

We need to be careful here. The text is not saying that this or that natural disaster is a judgment on this or that specific sin. The people of Pompeii were not worse sinners than those in a nearby village who escaped the lava flow. That was the cruel mistake made by Eliphaz in the book of Job when, trying to persuade innocent Job of his sinfulness, he asks, "Who that was innocent ever perished?" (Job 4:7). Jesus corrected this way of thinking when he reminded his listeners that the eighteen people tragically killed when the tower of Siloam (perhaps part of a Roman aqueduct) fell on them were not worse offenders than anyone else (Luke 13:4). "However," Jesus continued, "unless you repent you will all perish just as they did." Jesus uses the tragic event as a call to repentance. He foresaw that if the Jewish people of his time continued in their current ways—seeking their own political kingdom rather than the kingdom of God—they would perish. And indeed, they were overrun by a Roman invasion; many of their lives, their country, and Jerusalem with its temple treasures would be no more. In John's vision of the trumpets, he is *not* saying "God is going to destroy one-third of the earth." He *is* saying that his vision of devastating events, some of them natural disasters, is a picture of the horrors that might happen to creation and to people if they do not turn from godless ways and if evil powers are released and not restrained. Within this general point, however, there is also the sense, developed later, that in John's context the sins of the Roman Empire will eventually bring down upon themselves their own punishment and self-destruction. There is more going on in the spiritual world than you can see. We are facing a spiritual battle, and the only language which will shake you towards repentance and a change in your ways is the language of devastation, of horror, of invasion, of catastrophe; so wake up! John is here naming and uncovering the causes of this destruction and helping his hearers see the world "from God's perspective." As we think back to the seven letters to the churches of Asia Minor, we catch the sense there that even Christian people who have lost their way in their relationship to God can be contributors to their own painful contexts and receive their own rebukes from the Risen Jesus.

3. Echoes of the Plagues of Egypt

In the first four trumpet calls, there are unmistakable echoes of the plagues of Egypt described in the Book of Exodus. It is worth pausing to recall what was going on then, for both here and elsewhere in the Book of Revelation, John very much has Exodus in mind.

The story is that the Israelites are slaves of Pharaoh in Egypt, and God shows to them his particular compassion for the poor and oppressed. God raises up Moses to be a leader, to deliver God's people from their slavery, and lead them to a new life. They are to be God's new people in a new land. God's people are special to God. God's purposes for the whole of creation were tied up with their lives and their future (Exod 9:16). In fact, after their freedom, Moses and the Israelites sang a song of liberation, ending with "the Lord will reign for ever and ever." It is a song that John on Patmos makes his own later on in the Book of Revelation (Rev 15:3). But back to Exodus: God had given his people life and fruitfulness to thrive and multiply (Exod 1:7). But they were Pharaoh's slaves. Pharaoh stands for all that is anti-creation, anti-health, anti-life. He is the power that seeks to subvert God's purposes for God's creation and God's people. Pharaoh rejects Moses' words from God, "Let my people go." So, there is a series of "signs and wonders": plagues that are portents of God's warnings to Pharaoh. In effect God says, "Look what your evil ways are doing not only to my people, but to the whole of my creation!" Plagues are God's ways of allowing the results of sin and evil to take their course, so that people may be led to change their ways. God gives even Pharaoh and his Egyptians the chance to repent and return to the Lord.

Creation Awry

When we read in Exodus about the signs and portents of frogs and dust and gnats and swarms of flies, of diseases afflicting the livestock and the horses, the festering boils, the thunder and the hail that ruined the harvests, the locusts and the darkness over all the land, we are reading about creation gone awry. This is not the good creation God made it to be! This is not the creation symbolized by the four living creatures before the throne of heaven worshiping God. This is not the creation of which Jesus Christ is the first born, nor the creation before God's throne singing God's praise. This is what happens when people do not live according to God's law and God's will—indeed, when people live beyond their God-given boundaries—when God's world is misused, devastated by forces of anti-creation, anti-health, anti-life. This is God's good creation infected by evil: creation gone awry. This is the world that Pharaoh is destroying, but which God loves and is purposing to re-create and make new.

The story of the Exodus is the deliverance of God's people from the forces of destruction, from the hand of the tyrannical demonic power of Pharaoh, who thought he could take on the Living God. It is also the story of freedom for God's people, of a new life in the promised land, and a life in which Israel is to be a witness to all nations of how it is to live according to God's will and God's ways.

So when John on the island of Patmos hears, in his vision, the first four angels' trumpets sounding, the troubles of his world call to mind the plagues of Pharaoh's Egypt. He uses these signs and symbols of disaster to describe the sufferings of his own time. He tells us that the polluted rivers are poisoned with Wormwood, a name he copies from Jeremiah (9:15). And he tells us that he saw a great mountain burning with fire and falling into the sea, another image which John takes from Jeremiah, an image that comes again later in the Book of Revelation. In Jeremiah's prophecy, the message is of the total destruction of the great city of Babylon (Jer 51:24–30), where God's people had been held in exile centuries before. "Babylon" becomes John's chosen name for Rome (in chapter 17 we meet the prostitute in scarlet, who carries the name of "Babylon the Great"; she is seated on "seven hills" which are the hills of Rome: this all comes a bit clearer in our next chapter). "Babylon" comes to stand for human society organized without reference to God. It stands for the kingdom of this world over against the kingdom of God. The plagues in Revelation are, like the plagues at the time of the Exodus, God's ways of allowing the results of sin and evil to take their course, exposing the effects of human Empire, idolatry, and injustice. The other thing that John makes clear is that, awful though it is, God's judgment is restrained. That is probably what John means by saying that only "a third" of the earth is affected. God holds back the forces of destruction to allow opportunity for change of heart and for turning back to God.

4. God's Judgment Today?

Maybe we can hear these four trumpets sounding today when we read of wildfires and floods, more and more extreme weather events, drought on the earth, spreading disease, mass extinction of species, and all the unpredictable effects of human-induced climate change. Since the industrial revolution (with all its huge benefits), and especially in our lifetime, most of the ecological degradation we are experiencing has been caused by us.

The early industrialists did not know that by burning fossil fuels, by some aspects of industrial agriculture, by cutting down rain forests, we are putting a blanket round the earth which is leading to potentially catastrophic climate change. But we do know now. There is a responsibility on our generation to hear and respond to the warning trumpets. But again, we need to be careful. The people of California are not worse sinners than anyone else because the wildfires are destroying so much in their canyons. Their devastating fires are not the judgment of God specifically against the Californian fire department. And yet we humans are responsible for much of the current degradation of God's earth. Even in generations before our time, some Christian writers were arguing that a degrading of creation can be caused by human greed. And even longer ago still, in the eighth century BC, some of the prophets of Israel were also understanding ecological devastation as a sign of divine judgment against human sin.

Isaiah, for example, writes:

> The earth dries up and withers,
> the world languishes and withers;
> the heavens languish together with the earth.
> The earth lies polluted under its inhabitants;
> for they have transgressed laws, violated the statutes,
> broken the everlasting covenant. (Isa 24:4–5)

Isaiah's near contemporary Amos had very strong things to say about the way the rich amassed wealth at the expense of the poor, about the unjust ways in which the disadvantaged people were treated, and that even the judiciary were not trustworthy. He describes God saying:

> I withheld rain from you . . .
> I struck you with blight and mildew;
> I laid waste your gardens and your vineyards
> the locusts devoured your fig trees and your olive trees;
> Yet you did not return to me, says the Lord. (Amos 4:7, 9)

So maybe God could be saying to us: unless you human beings live within the physical God-given boundaries of your finite planet, and the moral boundaries of God's will; unless you change your economic priorities, and your ways of producing energy, and stop cutting down rain forests, and so on, there are going to be more and more fires and floods and deserts and food shortages, and diseases and deaths and mass migrations. Wake up! Listen to the trumpets!

Environmental devastation should be a word to us to listen to the watchmen and the prophets (climate scientists) of our time. In 2012, the Christian charity Operation Noah published the Ash Wednesday Declaration called "Climate Change and the Purposes of God: A Call to the Church."[1] It spoke of God's joy in creation, the call to repentance, the claims of justice and love, and the possibility of hope in God. It quoted Jeremiah 6:17: "I appointed watchmen over you and said: Listen to the sound of the trumpet." It continued:

> In recent decades, and with increasing urgency, climate scientists have warned of the dangers of catastrophic climate change resulting from human activity. Instability in weather systems is already bringing destruction and suffering to millions of people. In the light of the best knowledge we have, climate change could result in the loss of livelihoods and sometimes life for huge numbers of people and the extinction of countless species.[2]

Professor Mary Grey commented on this: "For Christians, the themes of this statement—joy, repentance, justice, hope and so on—are not optional: they are at the heart of our identity as Church. We will encounter them in the form of a question when we face God's judgment: 'What did you do to cherish my creation in its hour of danger?'"[3]

Recently, the sense of a "climate emergency," and indeed an emergency in the loss of biodiversity, have become headline news, partly through Sir David Attenborough's TV programs; partly through the bravery of a sixteen-year-old Swedish schoolgirl

1. Operation Noah, "Climate Change."
2. Operation Noah, "Climate Change."
3. Mary Grey, personal communication to the author.

called Greta Thunberg;[4] partly through protest movements such as Extinction Rebellion. The lack of political will to respond to such headlines betrays a deafness in many political leaders to the loud trumpets of warning that are being sounded.

5. Three Cries of "Woe!" from God's Eagle

One of the reasons we know that the plagues John sees in his vision are warnings is that God's eagle tells us so. The eagle cries out to what he calls the inhabitants of earth, "Woe, woe, woe! to the inhabitants of the earth" (8:13). The "inhabitants of earth" means not everyone who lives, but those who live on earth as though there is no heaven, those who live without reference to God. Remember John's Gospel: "the world was made through him, yet the world knew him not." The "woe, woe, woe" from the eagle is a lament from a suffering God: "alas! alas! alas!" It is a warning that trumpets five and six will be even worse, but the purpose is the same: to call people to turn back to God. The eagle is sometimes a picture of God's protective wings (Deut 32:11; Isa 40:31). These "woes" from the eagle tell us of God's compassion and concern—as well as warnings to wake up and change our ways.

In all the misery of the plagues, we need to remember what John is doing. He is not writing a political manifesto against Imperial Rome—or Babylon, as he calls the great city. He is writing for fellow Christians who are suffering, sometimes persecuted, sometimes even facing martyrdom for their faith, sometimes bewildered and led astray. He is writing to encourage them to hold fast with patient endurance, and also provoking them to wake up out of complacency. John is also "unveiling" the ways that God's judgment works in history. God sometimes allows the effects of evil and of sin to work themselves out, so that ultimately they self-destruct. The eagle is calling, "Woe!"; God says, "Alas!"

4. Thunberg, "If world leaders choose to fail us."

6. The Fifth Trumpet Releases the Demon-Locusts (9:1–12)

When the fifth angel's trumpet sounds, we learn what is really going on, and it is not at all pleasant! The shaft to the bottomless pit is opened, and out comes smoke filled with mega-locusts. Locusts must have been a very strong image, creating a sense of devastation and fear. They are yet another reminder of the plagues of Egypt—but this time we are told they are demon-locusts coming out of the pit of hell which symbolizes the source of all that is evil, anti-creation, and anti-life. The abyss stands for the wellspring of the forces of evil which have infected human beings. They can stand today for the forces which we cannot control but which cause among people and societies devastation and the worst sorts of fears that we can imagine. The demon-locusts even have a king (9:11), whose name means "Destroyer," who is behind the terrors and the tortures. In fact, "Apollyon" almost certainly refers to the Roman Emperor Domitian, who thought of himself as an incarnation of the Greek god Apollo. John is painting a horrible and fearful picture of what God allows to happen when evil is not restrained. He suggests that God uses even the forces of evil—the demon king of the locusts—as instruments of God's judgment against all evil. This is another vivid image of the kingdom of this world over against the kingdom of God. We could include the demon-locusts among those who are later called "the destroyers of the earth" (11:18).

Are we right to see here allusions to the coercive power of Empire? It would, of course, be fanciful and foolish (though too many Christians have tried) to suggest that this horseman, or this plague, or this locust swarm corresponds to one specific political event, or even person, in today's world. John did not know anything about climate change, or the free market economy, or nuclear weapons. We can, though, look with anxiety—with John's vision in our minds—on today's global powers of energy production and distribution, on the powerful hold of the consumer economy, on the power of agribusinesses behind the loss of rain forests, on the global arms races, and so on. Global powers are at work, sometimes as destructive of human well-being and creation's well-being as a cloud of devouring locusts.

7. The Sixth Trumpet Sets Free an Invading Cavalry (9:13–21)

As the sixth trumpet sounds, John now hears a voice "coming from the horns of the golden altar." John first writes about the golden altar in chapter 8, where we discovered that God takes the prayers of his people, sets them ablaze with heavenly fire, and casts the powerful mix onto the earth. Perhaps this trumpet call is part of the answer to those prayers, but it is not what they were expecting. There is a huge invasion of a demonic cavalry, led by four destroying angels, and more plagues. They sound very much like the Parthian army, who had a cavalry with armor for their soldiers and their horses. The Parthians had been at war with their Roman neighbors for many years, with territory like Armenia changing hands as each empire took the ascendency. The Parthians—like the locusts—caused fear among John's contemporaries. They occupied most of what we now know as Iran, and as far even as parts of Pakistan. Their border with Roman Empire was the Euphrates River where John's vision sees that four angels had been on duty apparently holding back further human violence, until now. God has had different ways of bringing about his judgment in history, in this case by allowing more of the destroyers of the earth, which are evil powers opposed to God, to burn themselves out by doing their worst. The invading cavalry is John's image for the spread of evil in the world of empires, where no one without the love of God is safe. Tom Wright comments on this passage:

> The whole world, though made by God and loved by God, has come to harbor within it such rebellion, such anti-creation destructiveness, that, though God normally requires it to be restrained, if it is to be dealt with

Jesus Is King of All Creation

it must, sooner or later, be allowed to come out, to show itself in its true colors.[5]

Yet, says John, the people of the world (that is, those who are not the redeemed people of God) still did not

> repent of the work of their hands; they did not stop worshiping demons, and idols of gold, silver, bronze, stone and wood . . . nor did they repent of their murders, their magic arts, their sexual immorality or their thefts. (Rev 9:20)

Just as Pharaoh refused to repent in the face of the plagues of his time, locusts among them, so some of the people of John's time were unrepentant and found themselves caught up into this catalogue of the evils and sins of the empire. It is in contexts of horrors such as this that we need to hold on to the wonderful words of St. Paul that "neither death, nor life, nor angels, nor rulers, nor height, nor depth, nor anything else in all creation will be able to separate us from the love of God in Christ Jesus our Lord" (Rom 8:38–39).

All through this series of trumpets, there are two emphases: first, the sovereign rule of God against the godless powers of evil, seen sometimes in the ecological crises that affect God's earth; and second, the call to people to change their ways while there is still opportunity. John is underlining to the churches of his day that there will be opposition to their faith that can lead to suffering and even to death, and he is urging them to wake up to what is going on.

8. An Interlude

We now come to Revelation chapters 10 and 11; two chapters of an interlude between the sounding of the sixth trumpet and the final blast of the seventh trumpet. Before we reach that Last Trumpet, which signals the coming Day of the Lord, there are more words for the churches.

5. Wright, *Revelation*, 86.

a. The Angel with the Little Scroll (10:1–11)

First appears a mighty angel, towering over land and sea, looking a bit like the Risen Jesus, and with a rainbow over his head. It provides a reminder that even in the middle of judgment, God never forgets his promise of mercy, and his covenant with the whole of creation. The angel's words underline for us that the whole earth is God's good creation. The angel swears by "him who lives for ever and ever, who created the heavens and all that is in them, the earth and all that is in it, and the sea and all that is in it" (10:6). There will be no more delay before the final seventh trumpet sounds the arrival of the Day of the Lord, when God's kingly rule is seen on earth. "In the days when the seventh angel is to blow his trumpet, the mystery of God will be fulfilled" (10:7).

The angel has a little scroll open in his hand and gives it to John. This recalls the great scroll of God's book of world destiny and the story of God's purposes that the Lamb opened in chapter 6. The little scroll must contain those same purposes of God—but now the task of bearing witness is given to God's prophet and God's church. It is a small earth-sized scroll, which is the counterpart to the sealed scroll in God's hands in heaven. John is to eat the little scroll and finds it sweet with the words of its message—an image largely taken from the prophecy of Ezekiel—but then it feels bitter in his stomach when he realizes that the sufferings and persecutions are to continue. The angel's word to John—and to the wider church—is "You must prophesy" (10:11).

The sounds of the trumpets are interrupted by this little episode: an open book and the call to prophesy "to many peoples and nations and languages and kings." The mystery of God is to be fulfilled through the human agency of preaching of God's word.

b. Measuring the Sanctuary and Two Witnesses (11:1–14)

In the second interlude as we await the Last Trumpet, John is told to measure the sanctuary of God's temple. This is rather strange, but it may refer back to either the prophet Zechariah or the prophet

Ezekiel, who both measured the temple. It seems that in both their cases this was something to do with making the place secure for God's people. This would fit with John's pattern of including encouraging words for the suffering churches while he tells his vision of judgments. As God's new people are sealed with God's mark on them, now the sanctuary of God is made secure for them.

Then there is a very peculiar section about two witnesses, which seems filled with allusions to all sorts of Old Testament themes. We are told that they "stand before the Lord of the earth" (11:4). The main point we are going to pick up from this is that God identifies two witnesses (who are possibly Elijah and Moses) who stand for all God's witnessing prophets, and they are to give testimony to the "inhabitants of the earth"—to the people who live in God's world without reference to God. This is a key moment in the Book of Revelation: it is through the witness and testimony and preaching of God's people that the nations can be brought to acknowledge the kingly rule of Christ. God uses his human agents in the outworking of the victory of Christ. The sad truth is that God's witnesses get blamed for the plagues which have afflicted the earth; they in turn are attacked and killed by "the Beast" from the abyss. Godless society seems relieved that God's messengers can no longer torment them with unwelcome truths and their calls for repentance. God's witnesses are never promised an easy ride: bearing witness to Christ can be risky and painful. The upshot though, is that the witnesses are eventually caught up to heaven with God. The signs of the coming of the Day of the Lord's judgment are made clear (earthquakes; the godless city collapses in on itself), and the perhaps unexpected good news is that some do repent and change their ways and give glory to God (11:13).

9. The Seventh Trumpet Sounds (11:15–19)

Now is the time for the proclamation of the coming Day of the Lord. This is the last trumpet, and in many ways it is the heart—indeed, the watershed—of the Book of Revelation. Loud voices in heaven cry out triumphantly: "The kingdom of the world has become the kingdom of our Lord and of his Messiah" (11:15).

All the struggles and persecutions, all the plagues and horrors, all the words of encouragement to the churches of God's protection, and the call to prophesy all lead up to this. The kingdom of the world—that is, the chaotic rule of evil and the violent power of Empire throughout God's creation—now bows before God's kingdom of truth and love, centered in the word of God's gospel and the self-giving sacrifice of the Lamb of God on Calvary's cross.

All the twenty-four elders—representing all God's people— "fell on their faces and worshiped God," singing:

> "We give you thanks, Lord God Almighty, who are and who were, for you have taken your great power and begun to reign." (11:16–17)

The Day of the Wrath of the Lamb is also the day of joy in God's kingdom. As we have said before, we need to understand wrath in the context of love. The Lion and the Lamb belong together in a demonstration of majestic power through self-giving sacrificial love.

With echoes of Psalm 2 and its celebration of the kingly rule of God over the raging of the nations, John continues to recognize God's judgment against the evil rulers of the world, for the vindication of all God's faithful people, and—note this—for "destroying those who destroy the earth" (11:18). Who are these destroyers? We have already met the horsemen of conquest, war, economic injustice and famine, and deadly pestilence. We have learned that the plagues, which include the polluting poison of Wormwood and the blazing mountain of Babylon, belong with the locusts from the pit of hell and their king, the Destroyer. We have heard the thunder of the murderous demonic cavalry. These images stand for the powers of evil which infect every part of God's creation and—as we shall see more clearly in our next chapter—find expression through the ideologies and powers of human societies organized in opposition to God. They are what St. Paul called "principalities and powers." The destroyers are anti-creation, anti-health, anti-life, anti-Christ. When God's Day comes and his new age begins, all these evil destroyers, like Pharaoh long ago in Egypt, will find their power destroyed, "and God may be all in all" (1 Cor 15:28).

There are strong echoes in this central part of Revelation of many other psalms, for example Psalm 98, which celebrates God's rule over nations and over creation:

> O sing to the Lord a new song,
> for he has done marvelous things.
> His right hand and his holy arm
> have gotten him victory.
> The Lord has made known his victory;
> he has revealed his vindication in the sight of the nations.
> He has remembered his steadfast love and faithfulness
> to the house of Israel.
> All the ends of the earth have seen
> the victory of our God.
>
> Make a joyful noise to the Lord, all the earth;
> break forth into joyous song and sing praises.
> Sing praises to the Lord with the lyre,
> with the lyre and the sound of melody.
> With trumpets and the sound of the horn
> make a joyful noise before the King, the Lord.
>
> Let the sea roar, and all that fills it;
> the world and those who live in it.
> Let the floods clap their hands;
> let the hills sing together for joy
> at the presence of the Lord,
> for he is coming to judge the earth.
> He will judge the world with righteousness,
> and the peoples with equity.

And there are reminders also of the Song of Moses after the deliverance of the exodus; the song ends: "The Lord will reign for ever and ever" (Exod 15:17).

10. God's Sanctuary in Heaven is Opened.

> Then God's temple in heaven was opened, and the ark
> of his covenant was seen within his temple; and there
> were flashes of lightning, rumblings, peals of thunder, an
> earthquake, and heavy hail. (Rev 11:19)

John sees that God's future now stands open for all the earth.
The temple on earth, so ruthlessly destroyed in Jerusalem by the
Romans, is still the sign in heaven of God's presence with God's
people, and it now stands open. The temple treasures, like the ark,
stolen from the Jerusalem temple by General Titus, are seen in
their heavenly counterpart to be kept safe with God. The covenant
is the eternal promise of God's faithfulness to give life and not to
destroy. The rainbow is the sign of God's commitment to all people
and to every living creature. All the earth now has a future under
the kingly rule of God. Now the whole earth will see that Jesus is
King of all creation.

That is a word of hope as well as warning, rebuke as well
as encouragement, in Ephesus and Smyrna, in Pergamum and
Thyatira, in Sardis and Philadelphia and Laodicea. You are facing
tribulation. Jesus faced tribulation for you and is now exalted as
King of all creation. Jesus was a Faithful and True Witness: you
are to be faithful and true witnesses to him. The call now is for
continuing patient endurance.

Joy to the world: the Lord is King!

Jesus Is King of All Creation

Joy to the world, the Lord is come!
Let earth receive her King;
Let every heart prepare Him room
And heaven and nature sing.

Joy to the earth, the Savior reigns!
Let men their songs employ.
While fields and floods, rocks, hills and plains
Repeat the sounding joy.

No more let sin and sorrows grow
Not thorns infest the ground;
He comes to make His blessings flow
Far as the curse is found.

He rules the world with truth and grace
And makes the nations prove
The glories of His righteousness
And wonders of His love.

Isaac Watts (1674–1748)

For Prayer, Reflection, Discussion

Operation Noah's Ash Wednesday Declaration, "Climate Change and the Purposes of God," called us to:

- Find joy in God's creation
- Listen to today's prophets (scientists)
- Repent and change our ways
- Take responsibility—care of creation
- Seek justice—in economic priorities; that all may live sustainably, and earth may flourish
- Love our neighbors—especially those in poorest communities and those not yet born
- Act with hope—in the faithfulness of God[6]

"These themes will come to us in the form of a question when we face God's judgment: 'what did you do to cherish my earth in its hour of danger?'"

—MARY GREY[7]

What sort of personal responses do you make to this question?

"You did not act in time . . . We probably do not have a future anymore. That future was sold so that a small number of people could make unimaginable amounts of money."

—GRETA THUNBERG[8]

What should our prayer and action be for those most affected by ecological devastation and climate change—the poorest communities, the marginalized, the disadvantaged, those whose

---

6. Operation Noah, "Climate Change."
7. Mary Grey, personal communication to the author.
8. Thunberg, "If world leaders choose to fail us."

homes have been lost to the sea, those without drinking water, those living on less than $1 a day?

" . . . hear *both the cry of the earth, and the cry of the poor*."

—POPE FRANCIS[9]

"O God, who set before us the great hope that your kingdom shall come on earth, and taught us to pray for its coming: give us grace to discern the signs of its dawning and to work for the perfect day when the whole world shall reflect your glory; through Jesus Christ our Lord."

—PERCY DEARMER (1867–1936)

9. Francis, *Laudato Si'*, 27. Emphasis in original.

4

Jesus Is Victorious Word, Faithful Witness, and Righteous Judge

(Rev 12:1—20:15)

WE HAVE BEEN INVITED to share in John's vision of the risen Jesus walking among the seven churches and of the crucified Lamb of God opening the seven seals of God's book of creation history and God's plan of salvation. We learned about the tribulations in the world of Empire caused by the horsemen of conquest, war, economic injustice and famine, and deadly pestilence. We have seen the signs of the Coming Day of the Lord. All heaven fell silent to hear the prayers of God's people in their tribulation. We heard the seven trumpets of the seven angels sounding their warnings to the worldly inhabitants of earth, calling them to see that the destruction of God's good creation is a calling for radical repentance. We discovered that underneath the politics of world history lies a spiritual struggle, which culminates eventually in the kingdom of this world becoming the kingdom of our God. Now, in the section of the Book of Revelation which starts in chapter 12, we come to another seven: the seven bowls of God's wrath poured out in judgment both to purify and to destroy. This underlines the point that world history is also the history of God's judgments against the powers of evil, and especially against that which is elsewhere called the prince of this world, the Satan, the Dragon. The seven bowls of God's wrath are God's final judgments by which, in John's vision, every power of evil is confronted by the Risen Christ, leading ultimately (as we shall see) to Almighty God's great white throne, when all powers of evil are utterly destroyed and God's liberating faithful love is fully revealed (chapters 21–22). Then, we read, "God makes all things new." A new people, a new community, a new holy city Jerusalem, in a new creation, a new heaven and new earth: all are filled with glory and worship and joyful praise.

We have said that the Book of Revelation is not an attempt to describe the future, let alone predict what is going to happen on earth. This is not a foretelling of future political events. It does not follow a simple chronological timeline but is rather a cycle of perspectives on the church, on history, on creation—all pointing to the Day of the Lord's Coming. It is a diagnosis—to some extent also a prognosis. Essentially, the Book of Revelation is about what is happening now. The distinction is not between past and future. The distinction is rather between what is hidden and what is revealed. The messages to the churches of Ephesus, Sardis, Laodicea, and the others are messages nonetheless also to today's Christian assemblies. The horsemen of conquest, war, economic injustice and famine, and deadly pestilence are riding in this world today as much as they did in Imperial Rome. The allurements and seductions of Empire—by which I mean human societies organized without reference to God, which become totalitarian oppressors, demanding the allegiance of their citizens, and with their idolatries opposed to the worship of the Living God—are real in our world, just as they were in Babylon, Rome, and the regimes of Stalin and Hitler. And the same demonic powers, embodied in human agents, still infect every aspect of God's good creation and twist it towards evil.

This is the world that we know. It is also the world in which the Lamb of God was crucified and raised from the dead, in which, through the power of the cross, the kingdom of this world becomes the kingdom of God. Jesus still walks among the churches giving praise and warnings and encouragement. It is the world of human history and of God's eternal Gospel of salvation. Here God's wonderful creation can still provide food for the hungry, living water for the thirsty, honor for the nations, and a community which is enabled by the "seven spirits" of God to "follow the Lamb wherever he goes" (cf. Rev 14:4). This is the world in which all evil will finally be destroyed, along with the "destroyers of the earth," and in which God will make all things new. That will be the eventual Day of the Lord's Coming that many Hebrew prophets foretold and to which John's vision has several times referred.

Before then, however, John's vision brings other things into focus, which he writes down to help the suffering churches. He is going to call them more than once to join him in faithful, patient endurance in their struggles, and to hold fast to their faith, the testimony of Jesus. In these chapters we are brought more directly into touch with the powers of evil. Here the cartoon monsters depict a horrible reality, particularly the Dragon, who uses the Beast from the sea and the False Prophet as its human agents. They represent for John the agency of the Roman Empire: its leaders and its propaganda machine. John sees the spiritual conflict going on behind the scenes. In fact, the conflict between the Dragon and God's messiah goes back a long way.

1. There Is War in Heaven, Causing Havoc on Earth (12:1–18)

There was not only war and conflict, persecution, and martyrdom going on in the cities of the empire and especially in Rome itself, but the spiritual reality is that there was "war in heaven" between God's angel, Michael, with his angelic army, and the Dragon, which is later described as the Deceiver of the whole world (12:9), the ancient serpent, the Devil and the Satan (20:2). We have met the Dragon before as the king of the locusts, as Wormwood the poisoner, as the angel of the abyss, and as Abaddon, the Destroyer.

Actually, John sees that the Dragon has been threatening God's cause throughout the whole history of God's people (12:1–6). John sees a woman, clothed with the sun, about to give birth to a child who would rule the nations, and the Dragon is waiting to kill the child at its birth. The woman seems to stand for the whole history of God's people since Abraham, and the child is God's messiah yet to be born, who will live and die within the history of God's people Israel, and whom the Dragon wants to destroy. But, the vision continues, God takes care of his child and prepares a place of safety for the woman. God's people have been kept safe through their past history. God will keep his church safe now.

But John's vision says something more. Not only was the war fought against the Dragon in heaven by Michael and his angels, but the Dragon and the Dragon's own angels were thrown out of heaven and thrown down to earth. There was a song of triumph in heaven proclaiming the victory of God's people—especially the martyrs—who are themselves called conquerors through the power of the cross and through their testimony to Jesus. This is their song:

> "Now have come the salvation and the power
> and the kingdom of our God
> and the authority of his Messiah,
> for the accuser of our comrades has been thrown down . . .
> but they have conquered him by the blood of the Lamb
> and by the word of their testimony,
> for they did not cling to life even in the face of death." (12:10–11)

This is another reminder that those who have suffered, even died, for their testimony of Jesus now share in the salvation and power and kingdom of God. The result is that God's people are assured of God's protection. But John sees that the Dragon's anger is aroused and understands that much of the havoc on the earth is the result of the Dragon's rage. The big struggles, political and social, which we experience between good and evil, between justice and injustice, between right and wrong, and all the temptations to give up our faith and our testimony to Jesus, reflect something of that spiritual conflict in the heavens and the Dragon left to do its worst on earth.

2. The Dragon, the Monster, and the False Prophet (13:1-18)

On earth, the Dragon works through human agents, human institutions, and human ideologies. Very clearly for the people to whom John is writing, the key agent for the Dragon was Imperial Rome (we know that it first of all means Rome because of its seven heads, symbolizing the seven hills of Rome). Rome's ideology and institutions are referred to by John as "Babylon." This godless Roman Empire is embodied in its emperor, probably Nero. It is described as a Beast coming up out of the sea (13:1). We recall how John often speaks of "the sea" as a symbol of turmoil, disorder, and chaos, and indeed, later in 17:15 "the sea" refers to "peoples, multitudes, nations, languages" all caught up in the chaos of Empire. Chapter 13 is a picture of a totalitarian state. All the people follow the Beast, they worship the Beast who claims to be God, and they acquiesce in the Beast's authority. This is a picture of totalitarian political power. Not that every state is always monstrous. When the state—even the Roman Empire some decades earlier in St. Paul's day—is providing the sort of social order and justice in which goodness can flourish, it is fulfilling its God-given function to be what St. Paul called "God's servant for our good" (Rom 13:4). But here in Revelation chapter 13, the Roman Empire has become monstrous, an agent of the Dragon, and has ceased to fulfill its God-given functions as a state. Now it is to be resisted: "Here is a call for the endurance and faith of the saints" (13:10).

City by city across the empire, there are local agents working for the Beast—depicted in John's vision by what he calls "another beast," this time "out of the earth," and later called "the False Prophet" (19:20). The False Prophet spreads lies, deceives the people, deals out the Beast's propaganda, and calls everyone to worship the Beast. All human commerce is then restricted only to those who carry the mark of the Beast on their hand or their forehead. (In the secret underground aspect to John's writing we discover that he identifies the Beast with the number 666—which can apparently be interpreted using the numbers to stand for letters to spell out the name "Nero." It is less than the "perfect" number of 777. And far short of the name of "Jesus," which, using the same method of interpretation, leads to the number 888).

This demonic trinity of the Dragon, the Beast, and the False Prophet is at work in the lives of people, their institutional structures, their ideologies, their national governments, their global corporations. They still fight against God's people and God's church, creating a false world of lies, of manipulation, of deceit, and of unrealizable expectations. There is spiritual evil power beyond human power here. We can get caught up into what Walter Wink called a "Domination System"[1] in which "the system" takes us over, and we seem powerless to take control over it. In our world, the market economy can become a Domination System, in which the economy loses its purpose to serve human values and the common good, and instead turns everything and everyone into a commodity. Wink includes among candidates for "Domination" unjust economic relations, oppressive political regimes, biased race relations, patriarchal gender relations, hierarchical power relations, and the use of violence to maintain them all. Many good and healthy aspects of our modern lives can become vehicles for Domination Systems, becoming our masters instead of our servants. Social media on the internet can become a Domination System, a power which controls peoples' minds and their time, but for which no one seems to be responsible. Sport, entertainment, and fashion can all become parts of a system that is used for evil instead of good. Racist political ideologies, drugs gangs, and associated knife crime can become parts of Domination Systems, with all their destructiveness. Some argue that the 2016 UK Brexit Referendum about leaving the European Union was greatly influenced by lies and by hatred. Certainly, many voters did not know what they wanted, and the temptation was constantly given to weigh everything in terms of selfish needs. Are all these examples of Empire?

While John mostly has Imperial Rome's dark forces in clear focus, the mark of the Beast falls on all totalitarian regimes and all institutions that become idolatrous and effectively demand the

1. Wink, *Powers That Be*, 37.

"worship" of their people. In Alan Bullock's book *Hitler: A Study in Tyranny*,[2] he illustrates what we have called the work of the False Prophet in its service of the Beast by referring to Hitler's patterns of creating mistrust in government institutions, his undermining of trust in the judicial processes, his constant critique of the media, and his apparent lack of any conception of truth. The Nazi propaganda had the mark of the Beast upon it when it was used to beguile huge crowds of people to follow every word of the Führer, even to the point of worship. We can also identify aspects of totalitarian government in our present world. The Beast is still alive and well, and we can discern its marks. The False Prophet is still deceiving the people. That is what John's vision describes in Revelation 13.

3. Jesus Is the Victorious Word; The Lamb on Mount Zion; The Eternal Gospel; The Song of Moses and of the Lamb (ch. 14–15)

In Revelation chapter 14, the mood changes. Instead of looking down at the world of the Dragon and the Beast and the False Prophet, look up! That is what Moses said to the people of Israel when they faced the wilderness all around them, the sea in front of them, and Pharaoh's forces closing in: "Do not be afraid, stand firm, and see the deliverance that the Lord will accomplish for you today" (Exod 14:13). So throughout Revelation John seems to be saying: You Christians in Smyrna or Thyatira may be hiding from the Roman persecutors behind your locked doors, but look up and you will see Christ, the victorious Lamb of God, on God's holy mountain, Mount Zion, the holy city of Jerusalem. The Lamb is leading his followers in a victory of faithful witness—even if it sometimes means death. There is a similar shift of perspective in St. Paul. Christians may be in prison, as St. Paul was at times, but was also "in the heavenly places in Christ Jesus" (Eph 2:6). The primary way John encourages a struggling church is to keep pointing them to Jesus Christ. So here in chapter 14:

2. Bullock, *Hitler*, esp. ch. 7.

> Then I looked, and there was the Lamb, standing on Mount
> Zion! And with him were 144,000 who had his name and
> his Father's name written on their foreheads. And I heard
> a voice from heaven like the sound of many waters and
> like the sound of loud thunder; the voice I heard was like
> the sound of harpists playing on their harps, and they
> sing a new song before the throne. (14:1–3)

Who are these 144,000? (Does 12 x 12,000 stand for the whole
people of God?) They are God's people who have kept themselves
pure, like soldiers ready for the holy war. The phrase (which is ex-
tremely uncomfortable for us to read in our very different culture)
"those who did not defile themselves with women" (14:4) refers to
the Old Testament purity culture (cf. Deut 23:9–10) for soldiers
preparing for war. "No sex before battle" seems to have been their
rule. In John's vision, these people are the elite storm-troops in
Christ's army. And in a fine description of Christian discipleship:
"They follow the Lamb wherever he goes" (14:4). What a thrilling
reminder of the triumphant witness and victory of Jesus on the
cross. While the Dragon and his minions do their worst on earth,
the Lamb stands boldly, victorious, high on Mount Zion,

Then, as a further reassurance to the churches, John sees a
"great and amazing" sight: he sees some of the angels of heaven going about their work. One carries an "eternal gospel" to announce
to those who live on earth, to every nation and tribe and language
and people. The angel spoke with a loud voice: "Fear God! Give
him glory! The time has come for his judgment! Worship the one
who made heaven and earth and the sea and the springs of water!"
(14:7). (This statement includes an intriguing reminder that "the
sea," which often functions as a reminder of the forces of chaos, is
nonetheless created by God: the creation which God has made is
good, but has gone awry.)

Another angel announces that the wicked city Babylon has
fallen, and this will be explained further for us in a later chapter of
Revelation. It is a vision of the self-destruction of human Empire.
Yet another angel cries with a loud voice about the judgment to
come on those who worship the Beast. This leads to yet another

call for endurance: "Here is a call for the endurance of the saints, those who keep the commandments of God and hold fast to the faith of Jesus" (14:12). "Keeping the commandments," of course, echoes Jesus' Sermon on the Mount:

> "Do not think I have some to abolish the law or the prophets; I have come not to abolish but to fulfil . . . whoever breaks one of the least of these commandments, and teaches others to do the same, will be called least in the kingdom of heaven." (Matt 5:17–20)

4. Jesus Is the Righteous Judge

John's vision continues with more angels bringing in the harvest of the earth: first a harvest of fruitful grain—all that has borne truthful testimony to Jesus; the nations who have come to faith in him. All these are gathered into the kingdom of Christ. This is followed by another harvest, this time of grapes which are thrown into the winepress of God's wrath—a symbol of God's condemnation of everything that is evil, a judgment against all that stands against God (14:15–20). Judgment is about making distinctions between the good and the evil, diagnosing carefully what is to be preserved and protected and what is to be put under the scalpel as something malignant, which must be removed. The righteous judgments of God through Jesus and the angels then unfold as we turn over further pages of this record of John's vision.

At long last we read of seven angels with a message that the plagues they will bring are the last, "for with them the wrath of God is ended" (15:1). We are being prepared once again for the approach of the Day of the Lord's Coming, when all evil will have been removed and there will be no more wrath. With cycle after cycle of John's visions, with seven messages to the seven churches, seven seals on God's book, and seven angels sounding seven trumpets, we have, from different points of view, been taken through the story of world history and destiny and have been led to expect the coming Day of the Lord. Soon the seven angels with seven plagues will pour out the seven bowls of God's wrath to purge the world of all that is evil and to reveal what damage evil forces and human sin and stupidity can do to God's good creation. The first four bowls are reminiscent again of the plagues of Egypt; the last three of the destruction of evil Empire and the fall of Babylon. All together form a sequence of judgments. They are all part of the persistent calling for repentance and a return to God. It is not that God is destroying the earth, but that he is using the plagues as a vehicle for his judgment against all the powers of the Beast and its kingdom. And liberation is in sight! Judgment is also grounds for joy, as the psalmist realized so long before:

> Then shall all the trees of the forest sing for joy
> before the Lord; for he is coming
> . . . to judge the earth.
> He will judge the world with righteousness,
> and the people with his truth. (Ps 96:12–13)

Now the vision changes again, with all the people of God who have "overcome" with Jesus standing beside a glassy sea which looks red with fire. Is this another allusion to the Exodus story? This time God's people have harps in their hands as they sing what is described as "the song of Moses," which is now also "the song of the Lamb":

> Great and amazing are your deeds, Lord God the Almighty!
> Just and true are your ways, King of the nations!
> Lord, who will not fear and glorify your name?
> For you alone are holy.
> All nations will come and worship before you,
> for your judgments have been revealed. (15:3–4)

The judgments have been revealed, all is now exposed, a clear choice now lies before us: yes to God, or no. Human responsibility still remains—and so does hope.

The "Song of Moses" is a reference back Exodus 15. The Red Sea has been crossed. Pharaoh (described by the prophet Ezekiel as "Pharaoh the king of Egypt, the great Dragon" Ezek 29:3) and his Egyptians have been defeated. The people of Israel have been saved. They can now start on their journey of liberation towards the Promised Land. How appropriate, then, that John should continue the Exodus motif and see the wilderness tabernacle (or the temple) standing open. The angels with the seven bowls of God's judgment against evil come out of the holiest place. God's hostility towards evil is part of his holiness The Holy of Holies, a large cuboid structure, housed the mercy seat of God on the ark of God's covenant. On the Day of Atonement, after the sacrifice, the priest declared that God has judged the sins of the people, and God's forgiveness has been accomplished. Just so, centuries later, in the darkness of the cross, Jesus cried out "It is finished!": the work of God's judgment against evil has been completed. And now here, as the seventh bowl of God's wrath is poured out, there is a voice "out of the temple, from the throne, saying 'It is done!'" (16:17). God's final judgment against evil is pronounced.

The first four bowls of wrath have been poured out on the earth and the sea, the rivers and the sun, as we saw also with the earlier plagues announced by the first four trumpets. Even God's good creation gets caught up into the working out of God's judgments. The fifth bowl of wrath burns up the throne of the Beast, whose kingdom is plunged into darkness. The bowl from the sixth angel dries up the river Euphrates, and as it does so demonic spirits like frogs come from the Dragon and the Beast and the False Prophet—the demonic trinity of creatures that are the ultimate source of all the evil in God's world. Their end is coming. And just then the Risen Jesus himself surprisingly speaks into John's vision: "Behold! I am coming! Stay awake!" (cf. Rev 16:15)—and the forces of evil get ready for their last battle at a place called Armageddon—a place famous as a battleground, though here the name is used not to identify a location but as a symbol for major conflict. It is then that the seventh angel empties his bowl, and the earth hears the voice from the throne, "It is done!" Lightnings, thunder, and earthquakes are all signs of the coming Day of the Lord. Islands and mountains disappear in a cataclysm in which, we are told, the city of Babylon is broken up, and all the cities of the nations fall.

5. Babylon Falls (Rev 17–18)

From Revelation chapter 17 to the end of the book the story could be told as a tale of two cities, or perhaps—to change the metaphor—of two women. We are first told of a prostitute, clothed in scarlet and purple, who represents the wicked "great city" of Babylon. Then in the closing chapters of Revelation we find another woman: the Bride of Christ, the church of Jesus, robed in white linen, who represents another city—the holy city, New Jerusalem, coming to earth out of heaven from God. As the picture of the scarlet-dressed woman (the city of Babylon) fades, so the picture of the Bride of Christ (the New Jerusalem, God's holy city) comes into clearer focus, especially in chapters 21–22.

We need to think a little more about the name "Babylon." The city of Babylon, called the great city, stands in John's mind for human society and human civilization that has been infected by the lure of the Dragon and the Beast. So "Babylon" comes to mean human society organized in opposition to God. To understand why "Babylon" is an appropriate name, we need to go back to Genesis chapter 11: the story of the Tower of Babel. In the land of Shinar, the people said, "Let us build ourselves a tower with its top in the heavens and let us make name for ourselves." The effect was that God "came down to see," and the result was "confusion" (hence "Babel") and the loss of communication. So Babel in the land of Shinar stands for human pride and self-sufficiency. It stands for the determination to build up power structures of our own without reference to God. It stands for human civilization ruled by worldliness and godlessness. Crucially it indicates humanity's refusal to live as creatures of God's earth: the higher they build, the further they get from their status as creatures of the earth, dependent on God for life and the means of life. Many centuries after Babel's tower, Nebuchadnezzar, king of Babylon, invaded the kingdom of Judah and took many of its leaders off to exile. He destroyed Jerusalem and its temple. And he brought many of the vessels of the house of God back to Shinar and "placed the vessels in the treasury of his gods" (Dan 1:2–3). Babylon was sometimes known as "the Dragon's Den" with the prophet Jeremiah looking forward to God's judgment against Babylon, saying "Babylon shall become a heap of ruins, a den of dragons" (or "jackals," Jer 51:37). So "Babylon" comes to mean world power that worships the world of the Dragon and his Beast: a powerful, godless, and self-centered city. No wonder in John's day, writing down his visions, he used that title for Imperial Rome. There are many dimensions of Babylon still visible in our world today. The call to God's people, then and now, tempted by Babylon, is to "come out":

> "Fallen, fallen is Babylon the great! . . .
> Come out of her, my people,
> so that you do not take part in her sins,
> and so that you do not share in her plagues;
> for her sins are heaped high as heaven,
> and God has remembered her iniquities." (Rev 18:2, 4–5)

Once again John's readers hear a choice presented to them. Come out of Babylon, come away from the seductions and allurements of Empire, come away from the false promises of health and wealth. This is once again a calling to God's people to reaffirm their allegiance as citizens of the kingdom of God. Remember the dark forces underneath the idolatrous pagan culture that surrounds you. You are citizens of another kingdom, with another King; you are followers of the Lamb, wherever he goes. You will discover more of what all this means as the vision comes to its close, with its images of a holy city, and a holy Bride for Christ. There is always a choice to be made: come out of Babylon. As we shall discover, that does not mean "abandon the world." No, this is the world that God loves, and we shall see within the holy city all that is good of even the nations and the kings and the cultures and civilizations of the earth have their place there. Babylon is the idolatrous ideology of Empire—human Empire, human power and pride set over against God. Come out of that and live as citizens of the kingdom of God.

Babylon Today

A vivid modern example of the call to "come out" of Babylon was given in William Stringfellow's 1973 book *An Ethic for Christians and Other Aliens in a Strange Land.*[3] His concern was to "understand America biblically."[4] The Babylon passages in the Book of Revelation give him the language he is seeking. Writing of the world of the late 1960s America, of the Vietnam War, of the nuclear arms race, of the *Pentagon Papers*, and so on, Stringfellow comments, "America has become a technological totalitarianism in which hope, in its ordinary human connotations, is being annihilated."[5] He describes "the doom of Babylon" hanging over 1960s America. Stringfellow expounds what he calls the "parable" of Babylon in the Book of Revelation to describe many aspects of the America of his day. He contrasts this with the "parable" of Jerusalem, which, as we shall see in our next chapter, stands for the holy city of God's kingdom, God's family, God's new creation. This is how William Stringfellow puts it:

> Babylon is the city of death, Jerusalem is the city of salvation; Babylon, the dominion of alienation, babel, slavery, war, Jerusalem the community of reconciliation, sanity, freedom, peace; Babylon the harlot, Jerusalem the bride of God; Babylon, the realm of demons and foul spirits, Jerusalem, the dwelling place in which all creatures are fulfilled; Babylon, an abomination to the Lord, Jerusalem, the holy nation; Babylon doomed, Jerusalem, redeemed.[6]

Stringfellow sees Babylon as a depiction of every nation in this fallen world—although at his time of writing it was America that was in his spotlight. The call is to come out of Babylon and to look instead to the hope which the Book of Revelation also offers: resistance to the power of Death in the life-giving sacrifice of the

3. Stringfellow, *Ethic.*
4. Stringfellow, *Ethic*, 13.
5. Stringfellow, *Ethic*, 20.
6. Stringfellow, *Ethic*, 34.

Lamb of God, and the healing gifts from God which characterize those living in "Jerusalem."

How do we "come out" of a "Babylon" in which all the systems of modern society interlock in a net which encompasses us, and in which very often the choices are not straightforwardly between good and evil, but between lesser evils and greater goods, and in which no way open to us is wholly pure? This side of the Coming Day of the Lord, we are caught up in the ambiguity of on the one hand finding Babylon's seductions all around us, even as Babylon fades, but on the other hand of catching glimpses of Mount Zion, of the holy city, of the hope that lies before us. The people of God, then and now, are called to endurance, to faithfulness in their witness, to steadiness in their part in the battles against the Beast using the weapons of self-giving love, and to clarity about their allegiance. Yet this is always within the tension between life as it is "now" and the "not yet" which still points to God's future.

Babylon Self-Destructs

John's vision continues in a nasty chapter 17, describing the immorality and blasphemy, the impurity and bloodshed going on in Babylon in terms of a prostitute (cf. Isa 23:17 concerning Tyre) dressed in scarlet and purple, whose aim is to seduce God's people, "multitudes and nations," away from their allegiance to Jesus the Lamb—the one who is truly "Lord of lords and King of kings." Her purpose is to make the kings of the earth yield their authority to the Beast. Her temptations are very real; her ruin is horrible.

Lament?

In Revelation chapter 18 we have a sort of dirge, caricaturing the laments that we read in some of the Old Testament prophets, such as Ezekiel 27 and Isaiah 47. In Revelation it is a phony wail of mourning for the destruction of Babylon. John's report of his vision continues. But who is weeping and wailing? Firstly, the "kings of the earth" in all their luxury are lamenting the loss of their power. They had given in to the seductions of Babylon and "committed adultery with her." Secondly, the merchants of the earth who have lost their trade and wealth add their lament. They had "grown rich from her excessive luxuries." But they weep because no one buys their cargoes anymore—gold, silver, precious stones, many luxury goods, cattle, horses, even "bodies and souls of men." Thirdly, the shipmasters and seafarers join in. Their trade is on the sea, and they had themselves become rich from Babylon's wealth. The crucial loss they all feel is of trade and wealth. Their priorities above everything else were economics and commerce. Is that so very far from the various Babylons of our day? But Babylon proves to be very temporary and fragile.

> In one hour, your judgment has come! In one hour,
> Babylon has been laid waste! (Rev 18:10, 19)

Babylon, to repeat, refers to human society and world powers with the mark of the Beast on them. Economic power becomes an idol, offering a false security. It leads to the idolization of Mammon, which all must worship, and none may criticize. Babylon also puts the Beast's mark on social movements that become idolatrous, such as some forms of nationalism, or an absolutized populism, an unregulated capitalism, an atomized and individualized materialism, or the tyranny of an inhumane communism which crushes individual freedoms. The Babylonian idols are crushed "in one hour" by the wrath of the Lamb!

6. Hallelujah!

The vision continues as John hears what seemed to be the loud voice of a great multitude in heaven, saying: "Hallelujah! Hallelujah! Hallelujah!" After the first shout of praise, John heard: "Salvation and glory and power to our God, for his judgments are true and just" (19:1-2). After the second hallelujah, he heard "The smoke from Babylon goes up for ever and ever." And after the third, this one from the throne of heaven: "Praise our God, all you servants who fear him, small and great." Then the multitude of voices, like the sound of many waters and mighty thunder peals, enables John at long last to discover what all this has been about:

"Hallelujah!
For the Lord our God,
the Almighty reigns.
Let us rejoice and exult
and give him the glory,
for the marriage of the Lamb has come,
and his bride has made herself ready;
to her it has been granted to be clothed
with fine linen, bright and pure"—
for the fine linen is the righteous deeds of the saints. (19:6–8)

No longer the allure of the woman in scarlet and purple. John's vision moves instead to the Bride. God's saints, that is, God's church, who have patiently endured and have held fast to their faith and their testimony to Jesus, these are the Bride of the Lamb, clothed in pure white linen. Within the history of the church, Babylon is always on the way to self-destruction; New Jerusalem is always coming down from heaven establishing the community of God's family. This side of the Day of the Lord's Coming, there are always two cities (or, in the other metaphor of two women: the tempting woman in scarlet and the bride of Christ prepared for the wedding feast). One is being judged and taken down; the other being born.

Babylon self-destructs. A new holy city, a renewed Jerusalem, comes down from heaven. The Bride is a new community in a new heaven and new earth, united with God and the Lamb, and worshiping God for ever and ever (as we will see in Revelation chapters 21–22). Once again, John's images merge into one another, and the metaphors are mixed. Here (chapter 19), the members of the church are invited as guests to the wedding. Later, in chapter 21, the Bride is in fact God's people the church This is what the angel said to John:

> Write this: "Blessed are those who are invited to the mar-
> riage supper of the Lamb." And he said to me, "These are
> the true words of God . . . Worship God!" (19:9–10)

Once again, we are brought to the purpose of it all: the worship of God. You have read the messages from the Risen Jesus to the
church; you have seen the seals opened and recognized the Lord of
history; you have been reminded of the horror of the plagues and
have seen the kingdom of this world become the kingdom of God,
the lord of creation. You have now seen the power of the Lamb
bringing down the citadels of Babylon and heard the invitation to
be part of the marriage supper of the Lamb. This is where it is all
leading: "Worship God!"

7. Jesus Is the Faithful Witness

In the wonderful verse Revelation 19:11, John tells us that he sees
not just through the doorway into heaven. He now sees *all heaven
standing open!* A rider called Faithful and True (that must mean
Christ) is riding out on his white horse, described as someone who
"judges and makes war in righteousness." The armies of heaven
(that must mean the Christian church) are on their white horses
with him. Initially we are told "no one knows his name but he himself," which presumably means that there is always that about him
which is unknown and unknowable unless he chooses to reveal it.
Elsewhere in the chapter several names are indeed revealed. The
"Faithful and True witness" is how the Risen Jesus is also described
in the letter to Laodicea (3:14). Here he is also called "the Word
of God" (19:13), and he carries the name King of kings and Lord
of lords (19:16). He is engaged here in a war—but the weapons of
Christ are always the same; not the violence of Empire, but the self-
giving of the sacrificial Lamb, crucified and risen from the dead.
This is underlined for us by the robe the Rider is wearing: "He is
clothed in a robe dipped in blood." Most likely this is the Rider's
own blood: the symbol of his own self-sacrifice on the cross. That
is the weapon he will use in the battle that is about to take place.

The Beast from the deep and the "kings of the earth," who have been caught up in the worship of other gods and led astray by the lure of Mammon and worldly power—they fight against the Rider on the white horse and his army. The sword of the word of God exposes their lies and false deceptions. In John's vision, the demonic powers of the Beast and the False Prophet are defeated by God's victorious Word, and thrown into the lake of fire. The vultures gather around their corpses.

So the Day of the Lord's Coming involves the Revelation of Christ (it is a vision of his "disclosure," his *"parousia,"* his Coming) finally to purify the whole creation from the evil powers that have infected it, and to destroy the demonic powers that have held so much of humanity in thrall. Christ clears his way to reign as King and bring all redeemed humanity with him.

But then John sees something more. In a rather difficult chapter 20 (which has received more interpretations than anyone could ever wish for!), John sees the fulfillment of a promise about God's people that was made right at the start of the revelations. Early on in the Book of Revelation, John refers to the Risen Jesus: "the faithful witness, the first-born of the dead, who loved us, and freed us from our sins by his blood, and made us to be a kingdom, priests serving his God and Father, to him be glory and dominion for ever and ever" (1:5–6). We met the phrase "a kingdom and priests" earlier in the song of the four living creatures and the twenty-four elders around the throne (Revelation 5). There the whole of creation is worshiping the Lamb who is worthy to unlock the secrets of world destiny:

> "You are worthy to take the scroll
> and to open its seals,
> for you were slaughtered
> and by your blood you ransomed for God
> saints from every tribe and language and people and nation;
> you have made them to be a kingdom and priests serving our God,
> and they will reign on earth." (5:9–10)

God's purpose for the whole of creation involves this "kingdom of priests" drawn from every nation, who reign with Christ on earth. This is the final answer to that prayer that spans the globe, "Your kingdom come, on earth as it is in heaven."

The Dragon Bound

John's vision in chapter 20 sees the company of those who have died—especially including those who have been martyred for their faith in Jesus—reigning with him on earth. On one side of our split screen, the Rider on the white horse does battle with the Beast on earth. On the other side, the Christian martyrs are vindicated—already sharing in Christ's kingly rule—and the Dragon cannot touch them anymore. That surely is the meaning of the symbolic "thousand years": a vindication of those who have suffered and are now free from the Dragon's deceits. Part of the kingly rule of Christ over all things includes a role for his redeemed people. The reign of Christ has broken into this present world—supremely in the cross and Resurrection of Jesus, though it has often remained hidden. But now, as John has already told us, the kingdom of this world has become the kingdom of our God and of his Christ, and that kingly rule is becoming visible and known throughout the earth. Now it is still usually hidden, although we are allowed occasional glimpses. When the Day of the Lord's Coming finally arrives, it will be fully visible in all God's glory.

Before that, however, we also learn that the Dragon—that fount of all evil power—is seized and bound and locked away, and ultimately joins the Beast and the False Prophet in the Lake of Fire.

Throughout this whole Babylon saga, John seems to be facing us with choices. On the one side, to come out of Babylon and resist her allurements and temptations, on the other side to look up to Jesus triumphant on Mount Zion and stay with those who "follow the Lamb wherever he goes," ready to stand with Jesus, the Faithful and True Witness. He is riding out on the white horse to face down evil forces with the power of the word of God. We hear the call for faithful endurance and keep looking towards the Day of the Lord's

Coming when the holy city comes back to earth as God's dwelling place, and his saints will be "priests of God and of Christ and will reign with him" (20:6). The ultimate and final choice is between those whose names are written in the Lamb's Book of Life (20:12) and those who have stayed in Babylon.

8. The Great White Throne, and the Death of Death (20:11–15)

Eventually, John sees the whole of creation brought before God's great white throne (20:11) for the results of God's judgment to be announced: "and the books were opened." People are now judged by their deeds. What matters is what we do in living out our faith. That was the message of the seven letters: love, faithfulness, loyalty, integrity; work for all that is life-giving. All that is not written in the Lamb's Book of Life—all that is anti-creation, anti-life, anti-Christ—will be purged away. Death itself, we are told, is thrown into the lake of fire. The rule of Death is over. The reign of Christ fully begins. The Day of Judgment is also the day of vindication for God's faithful people in Ephesus and Smyrna as well as God's people of all places and all times. Jesus in Galilee had said (Luke 10:18–20):

> I saw Satan fall from heaven like a flash of lightning. See, I have given you authority . . . over all the power of the enemy; and nothing will hurt you . . . Rejoice that your names are written in heaven.

Judge eternal, throned in splendor, Lord of lords and King of
kings,
With Thy living fire of judgment purge this realm of bitter
things:
Solace all its wide dominions with the healing of Thy wings.

Still the weary folk are pining for the hour that brings release:
And the city's crowded clangour cries aloud for sin to cease;
And the homesteads and the woodlands plead in silence for
their peace.

Crown, O Lord, Thine own endeavor; Cleave our darkness with
Thy sword;
Cheer the faint and feed the hungry with the richness of Thy
word;
Cleanse the body of this nation through the glory of the Lord.

Henry Scott Holland (1847–1918)

For Prayer, Reflection, Discussion

"Come out of Babylon." (Rev 18:4)

"Economic growth is the aggregate effect of the quest to accumulate capital and extract profit. Capitalism collapses without growth, yet perpetual growth on a finite planet leads inexorably to environmental calamity."

—GEORGE MONBIOT[7]

How can your church best bear true and faithful witness to God against the anti-creation, anti-health, anti-Christ powers at work in our world?

Has your reading of Revelation affected your understanding of God's love, God's justice, God's wrath? What does it mean in your context to "come out of Babylon"?

> Almighty Father,
> whose will is to restore all things
> in your beloved Son, the King of all:
> govern the hearts and minds of those in authority,
> and bring the families of the nations, divided and torn apart by the ravages of sin,
> to be subject to his just and gentle rule;
> who is alive and reigns with you, in the unity of the Holy Spirit,
> One God, now and forever.
> Amen.[8]

---

7. Monbiot, "Dare to Declare Capitalism Dead."
8. *Common Worship.* Collect for the Third Sunday before Advent.

5

Jesus Is Lord of Life:
The Beginning and the End

(Rev 21:1—22:5)

THE APOCALYPSE OF JESUS Christ has many references to Jesus as the Faithful and True Witness to the everlasting gospel from God, and also many encouragements to God's people to bear their own witness—what is often called "the testimony of Jesus." This means two things. First, it means the "testimony from Jesus," which is the revelation given through the angel to John, who wrote down the report of his visions for the churches to read. But secondly it means "the testimony about Jesus," namely the content of that vision report, which keeps pointing to Jesus Christ, Son of God and Son of Man, crucified and risen from the dead. We have found that, at different places in his record, John reports:

- The Risen Jesus is the Lord of the whole church; he has dictated prophetic messages to his suffering people, to warn them, sometimes to rebuke them, always to encourage them. John had written about him: "He is coming" (Rev 1:7); and much of John's narrative points towards a Day of the Lord's Coming.

- Jesus is the Lamb of God, still wearing the marks of his self-giving love on the cross of Calvary. He has opened the seals on God's hitherto secret scroll of world destiny and God's plan of salvation. Jesus is the focus of creation's history.

- Jesus, God's Messiah, is seen to be the King of all the kingdoms of this world. All other evil spiritual powers that seek to destroy the earth and fight against God's kingdom are themselves to be destroyed. The Lamb is at the center of the worship of all creation; He holds everything together.

- Jesus the victorious Lamb, with those "who follow the Lamb wherever he goes," stands triumphant on Mount Zion, above the anger of the Dragon, above the totalitarian demands and seductive allurements of the Beast from the deep; above the lies of the False Prophet.

- Jesus the Righteous Judge of the earth sifts the good from the evil in his harvest field. He is the focus of the song of liberation from his faithful people. Jesus is depicted as the Rider on a white horse with the blood of his sacrificial death on his garments. It is the Lamb's Book of Life that is opened before God's great white throne of world judgment. He is the Lamb who is now preparing for the marriage to his Bride, the church.

The text which dominates the first paragraph of Revelation chapter 21 is the voice from the one seated on the throne: "Behold, I make everything new!" (21:5). As John's vision unfolds, he writes about a new heaven and new earth. He gives us a picture of a renewed church, the holy city. There is a new temple; a new creation; renewed nations; renewed people. They have a renewed mission and participate in renewed worship. "Behold, I make everything new!"

1. The New Heaven and New Earth

Throughout the Book of Revelation, we have seen God's creation—heaven and earth—twisted and broken through human sin and the evil forces of destruction. And we have also met four living creatures, representing the whole of God's good creation, worshiping the Lamb on the throne. We have read of nations and powers and the "kings of the earth" caught up in the lure and destructiveness of a mighty global Beast-city called "Babylon," and we have also seen God bringing together his people, redeeming them from the ugliness of worldliness, with their robes "washed in the blood of the Lamb," and building them into a different sort of city—a kingdom of priests to reign with Christ and serve and worship God.

And now John, in the glorious ending of his record (Revelation chapters 21 and 22), sees a new heaven and a new earth: this is God's renewed church and renewed people in a renewed creation. It is a vision of the ultimate purposes being fulfilled of God's love for the church, for all history, for all creation and for all humanity.

> Then I saw a new heaven and a new earth; for the first heaven and the first earth had passed away, and there was no longer any sea. Then I saw the holy city, the New Jerusalem, coming down out of heaven from God, prepared as a bride beautifully dressed for her husband. (21:1-2)

This final part of John's vision gives us an understanding of what the Coming Day of the Lord involves. This is the culmination of the angel's word at the sound of the last trumpet in chapter 11: "The kingdom of the world has become the kingdom of our God and of his Christ" (11:15). It is the meaning also of the loud voice from heaven when the Dragon was thrown down to earth after the war with Michael: "Now have come the salvation and the power and the kingdom of our God and the authority of his Christ" (12:10). This vision is the answer to the prayer that has been prayed across the centuries: "Your kingdom come . . . on earth as it is in heaven." John's vision is of the kingdom of God now coming to earth from heaven. It is the kingdom of God which brings to fulfillment the story of the church, of which Jesus is Lord; the story of creation, of which Jesus is King; the story of human history, of which Jesus is the Beginning and the End (22:13); and the fulfillment of the lives of all God's people, liberated to serve with him as kings and priests in the kingdom of Christ's glory. To pray the Lord's Prayer is to make a commitment to that liberated service.

2. A Renewed Church: The Holy City New Jerusalem

John sees God's kingdom as a holy city of beauty, light, and glory, coming down from heaven, bringing heaven to earth—in fact, bringing heaven and earth together. God's kingdom is not something we build through our human efforts on earth; it comes down to us from heaven, as gift, a covenanted gift, expecting the covenant response of obedient service. It is a city, that is, a community of God's people now gathered, as it were, on Mount Zion. It is the New Jerusalem. As Babylon falls and its powers are defeated, the holy city comes to earth. Here is the ultimate truth about the world: all the lies of the False Prophet, all the seductions of the Beast, all the material attractions of Babylon—all come to nothing and wither away in the overwhelming glory of God. Throughout the story of God's people, God's purpose has been to build a city, a community, a family of his love. As John puts it in Rev 21:3:

> Now the dwelling of God is with men, and he will live
> with them. They will be his people, and God himself will
> be with them and be their God.

This brings to mind God's words to Abraham: "an everlasting covenant, to be God to you, and to your offspring after you" (Gen 17:7), following on the promise "in you all the families of the earth shall be blessed" (Gen 12:3). So we may understand John's vision as a fulfillment of God's covenant promise to Abraham.

The first emphasis concerning the holy city New Jerusalem is that it encompasses the covenant family of God, God's promised faithful love, and our responsive, obedient service and care. As Isaiah wrote long before:

> I am about to create new heavens
> and a new earth;
> the former things shall not be remembered
> or come to mind.
> But be glad and rejoice forever
> in what I am creating;
> for I am about to create Jerusalem as a joy,
> and its people as a delight.

I will rejoice in Jerusalem
and delight in my people. (Isa 65:17–19)

The second emphasis is on the word "holy": "prepared as a bride beautifully dressed for her husband" (21:2). The holy city is for those who "wash their robes" (7:14; 22:14)—that is, those who have put away their old habits and sinful infections and been made clean through the salvation which God offers in the death and resurrection of Christ. The image in John's vision changes to that of marriage (another covenant word), and the church is described as Christ's Bride—an intimate and loving union between Christ and the renewed people of God. There is a mutuality present in the image of Bride and Bridegroom which qualifies the sense of allegiance when we affirm: "Jesus is the Lord of the church."

To speak of the city as a "holy" city gives some sense to two rather unexpected verses in this part of John's vision. In John's report, there is an "inside" and an "outside" to the holy city. Outside are those still caught up in the ways of Babylon:

> Outside are the dogs, those who practice magic arts, the sexually immoral, the murderers, the idolaters, and everyone who loves and practices falsehood . . . Nothing impure will ever enter it, nor will anyone who does what is shameful or deceitful, but only those whose names are written in the Lamb's book of life. (21:15, 27)

In other words, John is giving us a vision of the holy city of God's family now being brought to earth from heaven—indeed of a new heaven and new earth becoming God's dwelling place—but until the final Day of the Lord's Coming, there are still features of Babylon around. John indeed sees the holy city coming now, but there is still a "not-yet" of the complete fulfillment of the Day of the Lord. When that Day comes, the throne of God "will be" in the city, his servants "will see" his face, and there "will be" no more night (Rev 22:3, 4, 5). And so now: there is still God's invitation: "whoever is thirsty, let him come, and whoever wishes, let him take the free gift of the water of life" (22:17).

3. A Renewed Temple

There have been a number of references to the temple through-out the Book of Revelation. The temple—often understood as a microcosm of the whole creation—is the dwelling place of God. The Holy of Holies is particularly the place where God meets the people through the ministry of the priest, and from which the whole of creation is blessed. We have read of the fire from God's altar mixed with the prayers of God's people; we have seen the temple court measured as a means of protection; we have heard of the temple candlesticks—symbols of God's gospel witnesses. We know that the physical temple in Jerusalem was destroyed under Vespasian, and its treasures taken to Rome just thirty years before John was writing. And yet we have had glimpses of the temple in heaven, opened for all to see. And here in Revelation chapter 21, the whole of creation becomes a temple of light with its cuboid Holy of Holies, "like that of a very precious jewel." The whole of creation becomes the dwelling place of God, the place where God meets with his people, the place where God is at home. So John writes: "I did not see a temple in the city, because the Lord God Almighty and the Lamb are its temple" (21:22). We may see the vision of a renewed temple as a fulfillment of the covenant God made with great King David, when David first suggested building God a house, and God's response was to say that David's offspring will themselves be seen as the house that God is building. The covenant words, repeated in Revelation 21, were first spoken to King David about his offspring: "I will be a father to him, and he will be a son to me" (2 Sam 7:14). Jesus is the temple in the holy city.

4. A Renewed Creation

After the terrible plagues released by the angelic trumpeters, we saw what can happen to God's earth when infected by sin and evil. The "very good" of Genesis 1:31, and the initial harmony of the garden of Eden in Genesis 2, was displaced by a creation gone awry. Yet we have also several times seen the rainbow reminder of

God's promise to Noah, and God's covenanted faithfulness to the whole of creation. The prophet Isaiah had offered a vision of joy and peaceableness when the Day of the Lord comes:

> Instead of the thorn shall come up the cypress; instead of the brier shall come up the myrtle; and it shall be to the Lord for a memorial, for an everlasting sign that shall not be cut off." (Isa 55:13)

John has a vision of a holy city. It is a garden-city, a renewed sort of Eden. "There is no longer any sea" (21:1)—that symbol of chaos and disorder has gone. There is rather a new order of things, "for the old order of things has passed away" (21:4). The river of the water of life flows through the city (22:1), and the tree of life stands by the side of it (22:2). No longer will there be any curse (22:3). This is Eden renewed, restored, remade. Jesus is King of a renewed creation. God's covenant promise to Noah is fulfilled.

5. Renewed Nations

"The leaves of the tree [of life] are for the healing of the nations."

(REV 22:2)

The "kings of the earth" and "the nations" have not had good press throughout the Book of Revelation. They have been seen as collaborators with the Beast. They have been behind conquest and war, famine and death. They have made their wealth in Babylon and have been among those persecuting the witnesses of the gospel (Rev 11) and fighting against the Rider on the white horse (Rev 20). John was charged to "prophesy" to "many peoples and nations languages and kings" (10:11). And, as we saw, some of the nations were brought to repentance through the testimony of the witnesses (11:13). But now in John's vision of the new heaven and the new earth, where God is the light (21:23), "the nations will walk by its light, and the kings of the earth will bring their splendor into it . . . The glory and honor of the nations will be brought into it" (22:24–26). Once again, the covenant words to Abraham come to mind: "through you all the families of the earth shall be blessed." And this wonderful celebration of the best of human civilization and culture, lived in harmony with the rest of God's creation, is a reminder of the prophecy of Isaiah about "the City of the Lord, the Zion of the Holy One of Israel" (Isa 60:14):

> Nations shall come to your light,
> and kings to the brightness of your dawn . . .
> the abundance of the sea shall be brought to you,
> and the wealth of the nations shall come to you. (Isa 60:3, 5)

The holy city, the New Jerusalem, is the gathering place of human creativity and treasures. Zion is the gathering point of all the nations of the earth. Jesus is the Lord of history, its beginning and its end (21:6).

6. Renewed People

The faithful people of God, who follow the Lamb wherever he goes (14:4) have responded to the calls for "patient endurance." They have heard the promise of the Shepherd to lead them to springs of living water (7:17). And in John's vision:

> God himself will be with them and be their God. He will
> wipe every tear from their eyes. There will be no more
> death or mourning or crying or pain, for the old order of
> things has passed away. (21:3–4)

The followers of the Lamb, whom John has often referred to as those who "conquer" in their faithful obedience to Jesus, are here referred to as his "servants" (22:3), who

> see his face, and his name will be on their foreheads . . .
> they will not need the light of a lamp or the light of the
> sun, for the Lord God will give them light. And they will
> reign for ever and ever. (22:3–5)

So John's vision closes where it began. God's people will be a "kingdom of priests" (Rev 1:6), here described as God's "children" (Rev 21:7) and God's "servants" who worship him and see his face (Rev 22:3–4).

The picture being painted for us in this final vision of John, the prophet, is of a rich kaleidoscope of images which all merge into one great canvas of a new heaven and a new earth. The picture is of a holy city, New Jerusalem, a new community, who is the Bride of Christ. It is a garden-city with features of a renewed Eden and restored and healed creation. The new creation is the new Holy of Holies, the place where heaven and earth together are the dwelling of God with humanity. All the streams of God's covenant promises (with Abraham, Noah, David, at the exodus) come to their fulfillment in Christ, lord of the church, lord of history, king of creation, the true and faithful witness, the Lamb who was slain.

7. A Renewed Mission

As the reading of John's circular letter throughout the churches comes towards its close, what are the people of Ephesus and Sardis, Pergamum and the other churches—or indeed of today's church—to make of it? The seven churches of Asia Minor each have their own prophetic message from the Risen Jesus encouraging them to stand firm in their faith; to hold on to their first love; to avoid the seductions of the Roman Empire around them; to be whole-hearted in their commitment to the one who loves them. They are freed from their sins by the blood of the Lamb and promised a glorious heritage serving God as his kingdom of priests with Christ forever. They will hear constant reminders of God's kingly rule around them, even in their tribulations, as the seals are opened and the trumpets sound. They discover fresh perspectives on the dark forces at work in the idolatrous empire in which they are struggling—alongside reassurances that they, the followers of the Lamb, are protected by God's own seal and mark of ownership, and that the Lamb himself stands above the fray, triumphant on Mount Zion. They are strengthened in their resolve and their commitment to patient endurance even when persecuted and abused, to keep looking up to the Lamb as the Beginning and Ending of world history. He is the One who gives the present time its meaning and its goal. They seek in all things to follow him, part of his harvest of fruitful obedience to God's will and God's ways. God's people know that their names are written in the Lamb's Book of Life, so that they are protected against the wiles of the Dragon and its agents. They are, however, constantly alert to the call, "Come out of Babylon." As the decaying culture of the fallen world around them comes apart, they lift up their eyes and their hearts to the holy city even now coming down from heaven to earth. They seek to prepare themselves as the Bride of Christ for their even closer union with him through the Holy Spirit. They gladly receive the compassionate healing, comfort, and thirst-quenching water of life. They commit themselves afresh as living communities of the people of God to continue to offer prayers that, set ablaze by the fire of God, can change the world. They continue to prophesy to kings and nations with the words of the eternal gospel of salvation. They continue to work to stand against the forces of anti-creation released by the angelic trumpeters. And they seek to heed the calling to repent, change direction, and reaffirm their vocation as servants and caretakers of God's good earth.

All this affects God's people in their individual discipleship as followers of the Lamb; all this continually refreshes their mission as the corporate family of God's people to keep offering God's free gift of the water of life to whoever is thirsty. Instead of the rule of Death, they are followers of the Lord of Life. Instead of a kingdom of violence, coercion, pride, and the quest for wealth and power, they seek to frame their communities by the kingdom of God's self-giving sacrificial love, mercy, compassion, and grace. And their mission is rooted in their hope in the constant covenanted faithfulness of God. They will seek so to live that love, compassion, grace, and hope will dominate their service and their worship.

8. Renewed Worship

Worship is one of the ways we glimpse the glory of heaven and earth together. The Book of Revelation was intended to be read out loud in acts of worship. John has learned of the power of prayers when mixed with the fire of God. He has heard the calling to prophesy and preach. And he has allowed us to listen in to creation's heavenly choir singing:

> "You are worthy, our Lord and God, to receive glory and honor and power, for you created all things, and by your will they were created and have their being." (Rev 4:11)
> "To him who sits on the throne and to the Lamb be praise and honor and glory and power, for ever and ever." (Rev 5:13)

We heard the great multitude before the throne:

> "Salvation belongs to our God who sits on the throne, and to the Lamb . . . Praise and glory and wisdom and thanks and honor and power and strength be to our God for ever and ever." (Rev 7:10, 12)

At the sound of the last trumpet, the twenty-four elders round the throne responded to the news that "the kingdom of the world has become the kingdom of our God and of his Christ, and that he will reign for ever and ever" with their song of worship:

> "We give thanks to you, Lord God Almighty, the One who is and who was, because you have taken your great power and have begun to reign." (Rev 11:17)

Those who had conquered the Beast sang the song of Moses and of the Lamb: "Great and marvelous are your deeds, Lord God Almighty. Just and true are your ways, King of the ages" (Rev 15:3). Then, after Babylon falls, the multitudes in heaven sing: "Hallelujah! Salvation and glory and power belong to our God . . . the Lord our God, the almighty reigns" (Rev 19:1, 6).

Early on in the book, we hear of Jesus knocking at the church's door wanting to come in to eat with his people. Towards the end we hear of God's banquet: the marriage supper of the Lamb. The church members hearing this read out would surely have thought immediately of the eucharist—the communion with the Risen Christ through which God continually feeds his people; one of the places where earth and heaven come together in clearest focus. "Christ has died; Christ is risen; Christ will come again."

And the center of the worship of heaven and earth is a Lamb.

I cannot tell why He, whom angels worship,
Should set his love upon the sons of men,
Or why, as Shepherd, He should seek the wanderers,
To bring them back, they know not how or when.
But this I know, that He was born of Mary,
When Bethl'hem's manger was his only home,
And that He lived at Nazareth and laboured,
And so, the Saviour, Saviour of the world is come.

I cannot tell how silently He suffered,
As with his peace he graced this place of tears,
Or how His heart upon the Cross was broken,
The crown of pain to three and thirty years.
But this I know, He heals the broken hearted,
And stays our sin, and calms our lurking fear,
And lifts the burden from the heavy laden,
For yet the Saviour, Saviour of the world is here.

I cannot tell how He will win the nations,
How He will claim his earthly heritage,
How satisfy the needs and aspirations
Of east and west, of sinner and of sage.
But this I know, all flesh shall see His glory,
And he shall reap the harvest He has sown,
And some glad day His sun shall shine in splendour
When He the Saviour, Saviour of the world, is known.

I cannot tell how all the lands shall worship,
When at His bidding every storm is stilled,
Or who can say how great the jubilation
When all the hearts of men with love are filled.
But this I know, the skies will thrill with rapture,
And myriad, myriad human voices sing,
And earth to heaven, and heaven to earth will answer:
At last the Saviour, Saviour of the world, is King.

William Young Fullerton (1857–1932)

Jesus Says: "I Am Coming Soon!"

(Rev 22:6–20)

The Risen Jesus Speaks, and John's Closing Words (Rev 22:6–21)

JOHN'S VISION HAS ENDED. Now through his angel, the Risen Jesus speaks, and the Book of Revelation ends with his words, and with some closing reflections from John.

We are left with an image of the holy city coming down out of heaven, the New Jerusalem, a renewed community of renewed people within a renewed creation. As John writes, Babylon's influence is still there. But the holy city is coming: a symbol of God restoring this world now, and increasingly claiming the kingdom of this world to be the kingdom of God and of Christ. Throughout the book we are constantly pointed to the Day of the Lord's Coming, when Babylon has fallen, the Dragon has been destroyed, and Death will be no more. For that day we still wait and pray.

So the Risen Jesus announces:

> "See, I am coming soon! Blessed is the one who keeps the words of the prophecy of this book." (22:7)

When John heard this, he fell down before the angelic messenger to worship at his feet. The angel told him not to do this, but rather: "Worship God!" (22:9).

Jesus speaks through the angel to tell John not to seal up the words of the prophecy of the book. By contrast, the prophet Daniel was told to seal up the account of his visions—for they were for the distant future. Not so with John: "the time is near." Jesus says, "Behold, I am coming soon!" And Jesus uses of himself the description of God we read earlier in chapter 1: "I am Alpha and Omega, the First and the last, the Beginning and the End." or, as we put it: Jesus is the source and the goal of all that is.

John has his own final words for the reader, repeating Jesus' announcement of his coming, and speaking Jesus' words of invitation:

> The Spirit and the Bride say "Come" and let everyone who hears say "Come." And let everyone who is thirsty come. Let anyone who wishes take the water of life as a gift . . . The one [Jesus] who testifies to these things says "Surely I am coming soon." (22:17, 20)

And John's response can also be ours: "Amen. Come, Lord Jesus!" The book ends as it began—with grace:

"The grace of the Lord Jesus be with God's people. Amen."

Bibliography

Bacon, Francis. *The Great Instauration, and New Atlantis.* Edited by J. Weinberger. Arlington Heights, IL: Harlan Davidson, 1980.

Bauckham, Richard. *Bible and Ecology.* London: Darton, Longman and Todd, 2010.

———. *The Theology of the Book of Revelation.* Cambridge: Cambridge University Press, 1993.

Beasley-Murray, George R. *The Book of Revelation.* London: Oliphants, 1974.

Berkhof, Hendrik. *Christ and the Powers.* Translated by John H. Yoder. Scottdale, PA: Herald, 1962.

Bredin, Mark. *The Ecology of the New Testament.* Downers Grove: InterVarsity, 2010.

Bullock, Alan. *Hitler: A Study in Tyranny.* Harmondsworth: Penguin, 1962.

Caird, G. B. *The Revelation of St John the Divine.* Black New Testament Commentaries. London: A. & C. Black, 1966.

Calvin, John. *Institutes of the Christian Religion.* Library of Christian Classics 20. Edited by John T. McNeill. Philadelphia: Westminster, 1967.

Chesterton, G. K. *The Man Who Was Thursday.* Harmondsworth: Penguin, 1937.

Common Worship: Daily Prayer. Church of England. London: Church House, 2005.

Descartes, René. *Discourse on Method, and Other Writings.* Harmondsworth, Penguin, 1968.

Dionysius. «Dionysius of Alexandria on the Book of Revelation.» In *A New Eusebius,* edited by J. Stevenson, 271–74. London: SPCK, 1968.

Ellul, Jacques. *Apocalypse.* New York: Seabury, 1977.

Farrer, Austin. *The Revelation of St John the Divine.* Oxford: Clarendon, 1964.

Francis, Pope. *Laudato Si': On Care for Our Common Home.* Encyclical Letter. London: Catholic Truth Society, 2015.

Fretheim, Terence E. *God and World in the Old Testament: A Relational Theology of Creation.* Nashville: Abingdon, 2005.

Gorman, Michael J. *Reading Revelation Responsibly: Uncivil Worship and Witness; Following the Lamb into the New Creation.* Eugene, OR: Cascade, 2011.

Bibliography

Hays, Richard. *The Moral Vision of the New Testament*. Edinburgh: T. & T. Clark, 1996.

Howard-Brook, Wes, and Anthony Gwyther. *Unveiling Empire: Reading Revelation Then and Now*. New York: Orbis, 1999.

Irenaeus. *Against Heresies*. Reprint, n.p.: Aeterna Press, 2016.

Kraybill, J. Nelson. *Apocalypse and Allegiance: Worship, Politics, and Devotion in the Book of Revelation*. Grand Rapids: Brazos, 2010.

Monbiot, George. "Dare to Declare Capitalism Dead—Before It Takes Us All Down with It." *The Guardian*, 25 April 2019.

Morris, Leon. *Revelation: An Introduction and Commentary*. London: Tyndale, 1969.

Newton, Jon K. *Revelation Reclaimed: The Use and Misuse of the Apocalypse*. Milton Keynes, UK: Paternoster, 2009.

O'Donovan, Oliver M. T. "The Political Thought of the Book of Revelation." *Tyndale Bulletin* 37 (1986) 61–94.

Operation Noah. "Climate Change and the Purposes of God: A Call to the Church." Feb 22, 2012. http://operationnoah.org/articles/read-ash-wednesday-declaration/.

Paul, Ian. *Revelation*. Tyndale NT Commentaries 20. London: InterVarsity Academic, 2018.

Rossing, Barbara. *The Rapture Exposed: The Message of Hope in the Book of Revelation*. New York: Basic, 2004.

Schussler Fiorenza, Elisabeth. *The Book of Revelation: Justice and Judgment*. Philadelphia: Fortress, 1985.

Stringfellow, William. *An Ethic for Christians and Other Aliens in a Strange Land*. Eugene, OR: Wipf & Stock, 2004.

Sweet, John. *Revelation*. TPI New Testament Commentaries. London: SCM, 1979.

Tabb, Brian J. *All Things New: Revelation as Canonical Capstone*. London: Apollos, 2019.

Thunberg, Greta. "If world leaders choose to fail us, my generation will never forgive them." Speech to UN Climate Action Summit, New York. Reported in *The Guardian*, 23 Sept. 2019.

Torrance, T. F. *The Apocalypse Today: Sermons on Revelation*. London: James Clarke, 1960.

Wielenga, Bas. *Revelation to John: Tuning into Songs of Moses and the Lamb*. Delhi: ISPCK, 1969.

Wilcock, Michael. *I Saw Heaven Opened*. Bible Speaks Today. London: InterVarsity, 1975.

Wink, Walter. *The Powers That Be: Theology for a New Millennium*. New York: Doubleday, 1998.

Wright, Tom. *Revelation for Everyone*. London: SPCK, 2011.

Lightning Source UK Ltd.
Milton Keynes UK
UKHW020831130420
361614UK00006B/317